Praise

'Read this if you want to cut through the noise, understand the signal, and succeed in tomorrow's world.'

— **L. David Marquet**, retired United States Navy captain and bestselling author of *Turn the Ship Around* and *Leadership Is Language*

'Having grown up at the end of the original punk era in the 1970s, I feel I owe it a lot, for discovering the essence of individuality and conformist rejection. I've often thought the world of work needed a bit of a punk revolution. Blaire's brought that to us with a twist. Necessary rebellion, anarchic approaches to distributing power and an antiestablishment vibe that gives us a chance to remove the bland and grey of the world of work in favour of shocking pink, tartan and an attitude to restore the expression of difference. I'm with Blaire in the antihierarchical league, the positive dissent, and I'm with the rebellious shift to a new wave of radical opposition to the corporate facade of work.'

— **Perry Timms**, MCIPD & FRSA, founder & chief energy officer, People & Transformational HR Ltd, author of *Transformational HR* and *The Energized Workplace*, voted HR's 'Most Influential Thinker' in 2022

'A crisply written account of the big themes leaders need to consider about our modern workplaces, transformed forever by Covid, remote working and new tech like artificial intelligence. A thought-provoking primer for business leaders looking to get the most out of a modern workforce by moving beyond the tired, old strategies designed for Industrial-Age management.'

— **Dougal Shaw**, BBC journalist and author of *CEO Secrets*

'Business leaders have talked about the importance of humans, organisational culture and employee engagement for decades. It must now go from simple talk, to leading, to real change. In *Punks in Suits*, Blaire Palmer clearly spells out why today's leaders must grasp the nettle, and the questions they need to answer to leave their organisations in a healthy state for the next generation.'

— **Jez Rose**, behaviour insight advisor, keynote speaker and author of *Flip the Switch*

'In an era where AI elevates our processes, Blaire's book brilliantly reminds us that our most crucial role as leaders is to be profoundly human. She eloquently highlights the quintessential human skills that will distinguish us in today's and tomorrow's workplaces. This work is compelling and challenging; it's a vital blueprint for our role in humanity and leadership.'

— **Ian Hughes**, CEO, Consumer Intelligence

'Blaire is a beacon of light for leadership, busting common myths that surround many leadership styles and thinking. This book intentionally pokes you with uncomfortable questions which reach the depths of your soul. It's a compelling and perceptive read, challenging our yesterdays against the future of leadership for the next generation and after. Not just another leadership book, but one that gets you on track for change, backed with podcast interviews to help deepen the narrative and understanding. Every chapter leaves you wanting to change the world… well, the workplace anyhow!'
— **Kathy Sharkey**, HR director, Rexel UK Ltd

'Not many business books are page-turners, but this one is. *Punks in Suits* urges leaders to step back from the daily hustle of work and consider the mark they want to leave on their organisations and people. On your day of retirement, will you look back and feel proud of how you changed things for the better? Or will you have left that challenge for the next generation? These are powerful questions that Blaire Palmer asks us to reflect on, and it's difficult to resist the subsequent route she paves out for reforming how we lead. This book is not just a call to arms – it offers direction and clarity on big, messy topics that we cannot afford to ignore as leaders.'
— **Becky Norman**, managing editor of *HRZone* and *TrainingZone*

'This superb book, meticulously researched yet thoroughly readable, challenges leaders to find the 'punk' under their suit, who's willing to say what's wrong with an outdated system and do something about it. The rise of the 'nonhuman workforce' (robots, AI) means we must move beyond the days of seeing people as slightly unreliable machines so we can embrace what makes us truly human – emotion, purpose, trust, values, humour, the abilities to improvise and to collaborate – while also having a life outside work. Blaire brilliantly shows why leaders should be more humble yet braver in helping us all to create a more humane future.'
— **Neil Mullarkey**, speaker, author, co-founder of the Comedy Store Players

'In *Punks in Suits*, Blaire Palmer brilliantly challenges the status quo of leadership and organisational management with a refreshing and revolutionary perspective. Her insightful examination of contemporary business practices against the backdrop of a rapidly evolving technological and societal landscape is both enlightening and provocative. Palmer's call for a human-centric approach in the workplace, integrating empathy, creativity, and connectivity, is a timely and urgent narrative in an era dominated by AI and digital transformation. This book is a compelling read for anyone aspiring to redefine leadership, foster innovation, and drive positive change in the modern business world. *Punks in Suits* is not just a critique

of traditional business models; it's a roadmap for building more empowering, dynamic, and humane organisations in the twenty-first century.'
— **Oluwaseyi Kehinde-Peters**, founder of the Pan African Women Empowerment Network (PAWEN)

'This is a great book for anyone who is interested in changing the world of work and making it fit for the future. It explains how we still take a Victorian approach to organisations which now use technologies such as AI and smart supply chains and have embraced trends like remote working and employee well-being. This, Palmer says, has to change. This book is a must-read for anyone who wants to make work work.'
— **Rhymer Rigby**, journalist for the *Financial Times*, *The Times* and *The Guardian*

PUNKS IN SUITS

HOW to LEAD THE WORKPLACE REFORMATION

BLAIRE PALMER

R^ethink

First published in Great Britain in 2024
by Rethink Press (www.rethinkpress.com)

Cover image © Shutterstock | Flas100 and Rroselavy

Illustrations by Ben Hughes

🌐 www.benhughesart.co.uk

📷 @benhughesart

Contents

Introduction
How Soon Is Now?

We are on the cusp of a revolution in how we utilise human talent in our organisations.

The changing expectations of employers and employees, the long tail of Covid, the cost of living, challenges with the supply of goods, the climate crisis, geopolitical uncertainty around the world, and, now, generative AI, all point to one conclusion – the Industrial Age and the socio-economic foundations which underpinned it is well and truly over. What might have worked then cannot work today because operational realities have become so different that new rules must apply.

And yet, with a few minor tweaks, we still run our organisations and organise our people the same way we have done for more than 200 years. The same beliefs underpin how we think about people and how we use them. It's no surprise that we are experiencing quickly diminishing returns. It is harder and harder to recruit and retain employees. It is harder to engage them. We have issues with burnout. It is harder to squeeze out a profit without slashing everything right back to the bone. It is harder to get employees to trust their leaders. I will go into all of this in more detail in this book.

These problems arise because we are holding on to Victorian beliefs, attitudes and practices towards productivity, people and the role business plays in society when they are well past their sell-by-date. It is time – beyond time – to rethink how we capitalise on the innately human qualities of our people and how our businesses fit into society if we are to ensure our organisations can survive, let alone thrive, in this new world.

This book is a rallying cry. I'm calling on you and your peers to unpick your own Industrial-Age hard-wiring and rethink what organisations need to look like in future. I'm asking you to consider how to use the mind-blowing technology that is going to trans-form the capabilities of our businesses and what they can do, and figure out where human beings fit in these new-look organisations.

I don't think we've scratched the surface of human potential at work. We've been so busy filling our day with activity better done by a machine and operating by the rules of work that were invented in a bygone age, that we haven't even considered what humans could and should be doing instead. We need to do this now, or our organisations will soon be irrelevant.

The day you come face to face with who you could have been

Some time ago, I was coaching a senior leader who was recently bereaved, having lost a number of family members in a few short years. He told me, 'They say when you're on your death bed you come face to face with the person you could have been in your life.'

He had retirement in his sights two or three years ahead. As we were discussing how he wanted to feel on the day of his retirement, we were reflecting on how the death-bed concept might apply:

'On the day you hand in your company laptop, you come face to face with the person you could have been at work.'

This idea became our mantra – who do you want to be the day you hand in your laptop, with no regrets, having done everything you could to leave the organisation better than you found it?

As a Gen-Xer with perhaps another decade left of full-time work, I ask myself the same question. When I have nothing to lose because I'm shutting up shop for the last time, what will I wish I had been brave enough to do and say?

The day you hand in your laptop and come face to face with what you could have done and who you could have been, you may realise that you too had been concerned with all the wrong things.

Take a moment and reflect now. It's the last working day of your professional life. They can't fire you because you're leaving anyway. It doesn't matter what they think of you:

- What will you wish you'd done differently?

- Where did you sacrifice your principles because you were afraid to rock the boat or speak out?

- In what ways did you avoid doing what you knew was right in order to hold on to your position?

- Did you set your organisation up for success or did you maintain the status quo?

- What did you know wasn't working, but you didn't make it right?

- How did you pull back from speaking your truth to protect your power?

- What were you capable of? Who could you have been at work if you'd had nothing to lose?

The time is now

You have a choice. You can either collude with the current system, edge out of the door in a few years, collect your pension and leave it to the next generation to fix your organisation, or you can grasp the opportunity to leave things better than you found them.

That may require sacrificing something of your own power and influence. It might require you to swallow your ego. That is why previous generations haven't done it. It requires a deeper sense of purpose than simply working your way to the top and winning the admiration of your friends and neighbours. It requires a willingness to embrace discomfort, to give away the badges of success and invent a new way to organise, recognise, reward and liberate the people in your organisation and the untapped talent they possess.

That's now your job.

This isn't a book that predicts what the future workplace will look like and then provides you with the governance model and organisational structures to build it. This isn't an instruction booklet for some Ikea furniture.

This is a book that explains the kind of leadership that's required to open the door to an unknown, yet-to-be-invented future, to walk through it and to take people with you on that journey. It's a book that explains what you'll need to jettison – the beliefs, mores, habits and power – so that you and the people you work with are free to find a new way of working.

The biggest barriers to real change are the people at the top because they have the most to lose. They are the most attached to things being the way they are. The way things are, and being able to succeed in that system, got them to the top. Why would they change it now and give away everything they've earned, the prizes of being at the executive team's table?

Because, unless things change, and change dramatically, they (and by 'they', I mean 'you'!) will be sitting at the executive team's table of a business that's drowning. The more you try to use the strategies that worked in the past – efficiency savings, buying in top talent from elsewhere, another transformation programme, another culture-change programme, bonuses for some and performance management for others, re-structures, 'treats' like fresh fruit in the kitchen – the worse things will get. As we will see, these strategies are based on Industrial-Age ideas about how to motivate people and how to crank the handle harder. These ideas won't work now.

What you and your organisation need is to start thinking differently. In this book, I will bust the myths that keep us stuck with our broken model, pose questions which you need to ask yourself (and which you need to pose to others around you), provoke you to notice the ways you perpetuate an unhealthy and ineffective system and activate you to begin a never-ending process of curiosity, disruption and iteration. I can't tell you where your journey of exploration will end, but I can show you what's wrong with what we have and describe the qualities you'll need if you want to play an active part in designing the future.

If, on your last day, when you hand in that laptop, you are leaving behind curious, enthusiastic, brave, thinking, emotionally self-aware, purpose-driven people who are willing to keep trying to make things better, then that's something to be incredibly proud of. If they are so focused on doing this work that they barely notice you've gone, so much the better.

About this book

In this book, I identify six places to look if you're ready to rethink how we work and how we use people to the best effect. I start by exploring the impact of new tech, specifically generative AI – a field that's moving so fast that is it highly likely the apps mentioned in this book are already passé by the time you've read it. However, unless you understand the unique contribution humans can make to an organisation, you may make the mistake of thinking tech can replace people. I will explain why this is a dangerous position to take.

I then cover new approaches to empowerment and trust, hierarchy, rethinking the role of leader, how we instigate organisational change and the role of business as a force for good in the world. Finally I ask you if you want to accept the call to adventure and start shaking up the status quo.

In writing this book, I spoke to experts who have inspired me with their ideas on these topics. You can listen to those conversations while reading this book. Each interview relates to a different chapter of this book, starting with my interview with Kay Sargent which you can listen to now. Or binge them all at once – it's up to you!

You can access recordings of those interviews here:

https://punksinsuitshowtoleadthework-
placereformation.buzzsprout.com

LISTEN NOW

Kay Sargent is a director of HOK's Global WorkPlace practice.[1] With a passion for using design to transform how and where people work, she spends her days (and many nights) working with clients on workplace strategy and design.

Based in Washington, D.C., Kay leads project teams that solve clients' business and organisational challenges related to real estate, business processes, strategic planning, workplace strategy and change management. She collaborates with organisations ranging from tech startups to Fortune 500 companies to optimise their real estate portfolios and create the most innovative work experiences.

In this interview, Kay and I discuss work and location. Given that hybrid working and how to make it work is one of the first questions I'm asked when leaders come to talk to me after a speech, I wanted to explore the topic with someone who thinks about real estate and the changing requirements of space full-time. In this conversation, Kay explores how and why we gather, how to stop treating employees as 'potted plants', and how technology can help make workspaces work.

You can listen to the interview at **www. buzzsprout.com/2250059/13618085**, or listen to any of the other interviews here: **https:// punksinsuitshowtoleadtheworkplacereformation. buzzsprout.com**

CHAPTER 1

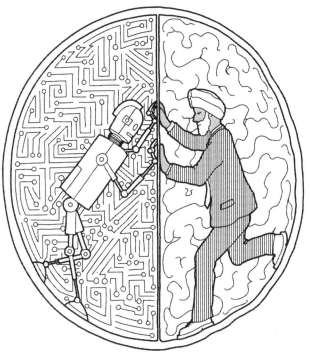

TECHNOLOGY

Technology
The Inhuman League

A 2023 report by the World Economic Forum[2] found that 85% of companies thought that the increased adoption of new and frontier technologies would transform their organisations. Big data, cloud computing and AI were the most likely technologies to be adopted in the next five years. Sixty-nine million jobs would be created, but there would be a decline of eighty-three million jobs in that same period.[3]

Employers expected a labour market churn of 23% of jobs, consisting of a mixture of emerging jobs added and declining jobs eliminated.[4] The report anticipated that 42% of business tasks would be automated in the same period compared to 34% currently.[5] In particular, tasks around reasoning, communicating and coordinating were expected to become more automatable in future. Around half of companies said they thought that this would create job growth while a quarter said they thought it would create job losses.[6]

Despite these predictions, I don't believe the future of work is bleak. That's because I don't think we have scratched the surface of what human employees could do at work if they weren't doing jobs more suited to a machine.

For me, it is most likely that tech will create jobs and make others redundant, but if we finally understand the untapped potential of humans in our workforce, there will be plenty of work to go around. That is unless the bots take over the world.

OK, not the last bit. Hopefully. But the sheer pace at which AI can evolve is mind-boggling. We cannot anticipate just how much it will change the world, but we can assume that, just from a personal perspective, this technological transition is not going to be a smooth one.

One of the reasons behind the growing levels of distrust in the world is job instability and the threat that new technology presents. What are these new jobs going to be?[7] What specialist skills will they need? What will happen to people in whole industries and professions that are no longer needed?

The technological transformation all around us may only be one of the influences on the changing nature of work, but it's a crucial one, a tipping point, and deserves some special attention because of what it means for how we work, the organisational cultures we need, and how we personally prepare ourselves for the future. As leaders, there are also ethical implications, not least the organisation's responsibility to those people it no longer needs.

Welcoming the nonhuman workforce

This new tech isn't like the tech we already have. It's more fundamental and demands that we rethink the 'contract' we have with the people in our organisation. Instead, we need to see the new tech as a *nonhuman workforce* working alongside our *human workforce*.

Whether it's AI, bots or databases, we aren't just using this technology to help us do our jobs. Technology is now doing at least part of many of our jobs. We are delegating jobs to AI that we would previously have delegated to human co-workers – jobs we thought were fundamental to the way we added value to our organisations. This tech isn't only faster and more efficient than doing something ourselves, it's cleverer.

I have been experimenting with ChatGPT (like a lot of people). By the time this book comes out I will be a pro and the tech will have moved on from where it is today, so forgive me if what I am describing seems 'so last year'.

There is a company I mention in this book. I could remember a few facts about it but not its name. Google wasn't helpful because the search terms I was using came up with a load of irrelevant results which I had to sift through. I then asked ChatGPT – 'There's a company, Brazilian, I think, where they changed the ways of working so that people had more freedom. I think the son took over from the father. Do you know which company I'm thinking of?'

The answer came back – Semco.

I asked for some links and it provided them so I could cross-check my recollections.

This is much more like talking to a colleague than searching Google. I ask GenAI to turn things I've written into bullet points or to summarise them for future reference, just like I would ask an intern or assistant to do some initial research and creative thinking for me.

This is just the start. At the time of writing, the BBC is reporting[8] that AI has discovered a new antibiotic that can kill a deadly species of superbug. I've coached numerous senior leaders in pharma over my two decades (plus) as an executive coach, and it's an industry that embraced big data before most of us knew what big data was. Now that big data is available for AI to mine for hitherto-unseen opportunities. It can screen tens of millions of potential compounds in a way that is just impossible to do with a human workforce.

The same technology can help us organise human employees in an organisation. For years I've been talking about the potential for more agility for human workers – for instance, rather than having a job description or being hired to fit, like a puzzle piece, into a clearly boundaried job spec, I've been predicting a time when a person is seen instead as a unique cluster of experiences, human qualities and expertise, being used in different ways at different times by an organisation, growing and learning and enhancing the full value they have to offer over time.

This is impossible when you are trying to juggle the complexity of what people have to offer on a spreadsheet. A human (even with the help of some clever Excel formulae) cannot work out all the moving parts.

Let's take 'Abigail'. She's a keen athlete outside of work. She was hired as a client services manager and is busy with three huge clients. Over the last two years, she's been on some leadership courses and is keen to develop her skills. She's a great listener and good at refining other people's ideas but she's not great at generating her own. She's having a few difficulties at home, taking care of her unwell mum. Her husband travels a lot for work. She has two children, one of whom is taking his finals this year. She loves to travel but hasn't been away recently because of her other commitments. She's great with numbers, follows Duran Duran on Instagram and keeps various Pinterest boards of what she'd like to do to her house if she ever wins the lottery (she doesn't do the lottery).

How do you work out how to use Abigail? She's a whole person, not just a client services manager. She is keen to grow and develop. Her personal qualities mean she has useful perspectives in all kinds of meetings, including meetings that have nothing to do with client services specifically. How can you, even with a clever spreadsheet, work out where to place her? You can't. So you give her a job with a job description which makes use of some of her qualities but not all of them, and which works in tune with her life outside of work in some ways, but not in other ways. Consequently, you've paid for all of Abigail, but you don't get what you paid for. She can add more value.

You have no idea what capacity she has at any particular time, so if you ask her if she'd like to be involved in a project you're launching, she may say no because she doesn't have time (or yes, even though she's busy, because she's excited about the opportunity and wants to appear 'keen'). She doesn't know if she will have time in a few weeks because her workload is unpredictable. So you don't use her. Instead, you hire someone else who will also be a fit in some ways and not others.

AI can help. AI can store and sift through all this information, along with similar information about your other employees. It can predict busy periods based on past data and other insights such as how demanding particular clients tend to be over and above the average. It can capture development needs and ambitions. It can design the ideal combination of personality types to be on teams addressing different kinds of problems. It can crunch all this up and recommend some team members to you.

It can then determine how much time it should take that team to deliver a result, and give you a realistic budget, based on data from previous projects. It can generate draft meeting agendas and timelines and let you know when certain people on the team are likely to be less used and are free to apply their qualities elsewhere.

And AI is much more than just this – it's your new project manager, your succession planner, your recruitment strategist and your finance business partner. With AI doing this background work, Abigail doesn't just fit into a puzzle-piece-shaped hole. She's bringing her whole self to add value to your business. She has a workload that blends with the demands of her life, and which can adapt as the demands of her life change. She can grow. She gets to use her personal qualities on interesting problems outside her narrow area of client services. Someone else can flex their muscles in the areas that she is weaker in. The tech anticipates future needs so you aren't scrabbling to recruit unsuitable people because you have a demand for resources and don't have time to find the perfect fit.

This kind of AI is here now. It's a brain – a nonhuman workforce working alongside a human workforce, doing work that is best done by a nonhuman and liberating your human workforce to do work only a human can do. Of course, your project manager, succession planner, recruitment strategist and finance BP will have to think about what value their humanity adds to the business when they are no longer creating Gantt charts and spreadsheets and populating fields in project-management software.

But what if these people are now free to think, be creative, reflect on the recommendations made by the AI and maybe assess the ethical implications of those options? What if their personal qualities, like Abigail's, are better used elsewhere in the business in a role that is hard to describe on a job spec but is much needed? What if, instead of just making people redundant, AI helps the organisation see where their true value lies?

Embracing this new world isn't as simple as introducing new technology and asking people to get on board with using it. It requires letting go of beliefs that determine the way we've organised people for the last 250 years, beliefs which have made us feel in control and in charge but which now threaten to hold us back.

Putting lipstick on a Victorian pig

The Industrial Revolution transformed work. Most of the norms we operate by in our work evolved during the Industrial Age. We clocked in and clocked out. We were supervised by other human beings who had been in the organisation longer. If we were successful, we got booted upstairs, changed into a shirt and tie and started to wield more influence.

Certain jobs were for women and certain jobs were for men – something we are still trying to unpick today. We had to prove our loyalty and commitment and play by the rules, and if we did that, we would continue our trajectory up the organisation, get our pay rise and bonus and, maybe, one day, a key to the executive bathroom.

Are things really that different today? I don't think so.

Because there are two Victorian paradigms that sit at the heart of how we organise and manage our people today. These two paradigms are so ingrained in our psyche that you may reject them, claiming we have moved on, or at least that you have moved on. Yet I see evidence of these two paradigms baked so deeply into the fabric of organisations, so inherent, that we don't even notice they are there.

These paradigms are:

1. **People are second-rate machines.** Machines are preferable. They are efficient and predictable. They operate day and night with consistency. They don't require 'handling'. They don't make demands. When they break, we fix them or replace them without fuss. But because we can't get machines to do everything, we use people. Ideally, people will behave like machines, and we will put in place structures, rules, processes and systems that create as much predictability, efficiency and consistency in how our people work as possible. We acknowledge that we will have to relate to people differently than machines, but we will do this primarily to gain more predictability, efficiency, consistency and, ultimately, productivity, from them.

2. **Most people are trying to get away with something.** If we give them an inch, they will take a mile. People are selfish and greedy. People are fundamentally lazy. They need to be motivated by someone else or they will do as little as they

can get away with. They don't really care about the standard of their work. If we let them, they would spend all day chatting, stealing stationery and inflating their expenses. Most of them aren't capable of making good decisions, thinking through complex problems, coping with pressure, change or growth. Senior, more sophisticated people are needed to supervise and control people, offering them inducements to do a good job and keep them on the straight and narrow.

What if these beliefs are fundamentally flawed? We have a whole system of reporting and accountability and decision-making, meetings, annual reviews, paygrades and job titles, job specs, promotion and compensation packages, policies, leadership behaviours, targets, competition between teams or branches or regions of the same organisation, all to keep people under control so they don't take advantage of our good nature and act selfishly, stupidly or with malintent.

What if people want to do a good job? What if they are just as capable as you of making decisions and handling complex information? What if we released the capability of everyone in the organisation rather than defining who is allowed to operate at a particular level or with particular powers that are denied to others?

And what would that mean for you? What would your job be if you let go of all of these outdated beliefs? How would it change the way you spent your time and the ways you added value?

If you're uncomfortable right now, you've come face to face with the reason the system persists. We may say we want to empower people, we want their fresh ideas, we want to encourage a sense of inclusivity and belonging, we want psychological safety, and say that people are our greatest asset, but if we fundamentally believe either or both of these Victorian beliefs, it won't happen. We will hold on to the reins just in case we need to grab back control.

The result is that our organisation is hamstrung. We've hired these amazing people and we then get in the way of them doing what they are capable of. No wonder there's a 'war for talent', high levels of burnout and stress, lack of engagement and a lack of ownership and accountability. Given the complexity of the trading conditions in which we operate, the demand to be constantly innovating and iterating, and the humanity we expect people to bring to their work (to care, to go above and beyond, to speak up and find solutions), we need a massive rethink.

Now we have the technological capability, we can finally unpick these myths about people so that we can liberate their talent.

What's striking about the pace of AI advancement is how many upper-middle-class, white-collar roles are 'threatened' by the new tech. In the past, it was mainly manual workers who saw their jobs disappear. It was largely a working-class impact rather than a middle-class one. Whether it was working down the mine, spinning wool, packing munitions into boxes or assembling a car, when a machine could do it, those jobs disappeared.

Many of those jobs required real expertise and talent. Bakers, telegraphists (sending and receiving Morse code) and wheelwrights underwent years of training, often through an apprenticeship, to learn their craft, but most were made irrelevant when someone invented a machine that could do their job. The upper-middle-class, white-collar employees in head offices made the decisions that made their blue-collar colleagues redundant but were largely protected from the advance of the technology themselves.

If you had a profession – doctor, dentist, architect, accountant or lawyer, for instance – you might adopt new technology but never suspected that a bot could do your job. We needed creatives as well – people to write copy, to do research, to make films and TV shows. We needed managers to supervise other people. We needed managers to manage the managers. Technology wouldn't replace us. It was a tool to take away the grind, monitor our activities at a simplistic level, keep us efficient and produce a paper trail of measurable outputs that allowed our managers to know what we were doing. Until now.

The WEF report estimates that 44% of workers' skills will be disrupted in the next five years.[9] Six in ten workers will require retraining before 2027.[10] You may believe now that a bot can't do your job, but I respectfully suggest that it will be able to do at least some of what you currently think requires your humanity to achieve.

If an ever-increasing number of jobs currently done by human beings will be done by bots, what sorts of jobs will humans be doing? Only those that require our humanity – our ability to care, to connect, to empathise, to invent and imagine, to create and innovate. The WEF suggests the most in-demand skills will be cognitive skills, creative thinking and technology literacy. Employees will be expected to be curious and embrace lifelong learning, resilience, flexibility and agility, be motivated and develop greater self-awareness. We will need to be as human as humanly possible.[11] That is because anything which can be done without these innately human qualities will be done by a machine.

But apart from the disruption and the job losses, that presents a problem for how we organise our human workforce, how we lead them and the 'contract' we have with them.

The intention behind treating people like machines is to get a reliable, predictable, efficient, machine-like business. You tell people what to do, and they carry out your instructions, just like a machine.

But when machines are doing the work that requires reliability, predictability and efficiency and you need your human workforce to care, to connect, to empathise, to invent and imagine, and to create and innovate, you can't treat them like machines, you have to treat them like humans.

That means dismantling almost every system and process in a business. More than that, it means rejecting those two Victorian notions that underpin these systems and processes and ways of thinking about human workers and replacing them with something else. Let's dive into that.

Belief 1: People are second-rate machines

The Industrial Age was all about efficiency. It was about the production line. That makes sense, because, if you make your money by producing a product, the more of that product you can make in a period of time, the more cheaply you can produce it, and the more consistency of quality you achieve, the more money you can make. Machines are great at all of this.

At the start of the Industrial Revolution, the capabilities of machines were limited, but as we progressed through the decades, they became more sophisticated and could do a whole raft of jobs that used to be done by people.

The problem was that, while there were still many jobs which didn't benefit from having a person doing them, it was a necessity because machines weren't ready to take on the task.

Let's take the typing pool.

In the early 80s, my dad became a planning inspector working for the Department of the Environment. He spent weeks at a time overseeing planning enquiries, hearing evidence regarding whether a proposed development should or should not go ahead. Then he would work from home (yes, in the early 80s) writing up his report and decision.

This was his process.

He would handwrite or type up his ideas, the various pieces of evidence presented to him and the regulations and precedents he would be considering.

He would then dictate his report into a Dictaphone. The tape recording would be sent by mail to the typing pool. Someone would listen to his voice and type up his report. The report would then be sent back to him to be checked. He would make any amendments and send that back to the typing pool who would type it up again with the corrections.

That report would usually be the official final version and the decision would be announced.

The human being typing up the report didn't add any humanity to the process. They simply typed. As soon as my dad got his first word processor, he didn't need the typing pool. A machine did the job instead and, apart from the wonderful people in the typing pool losing their jobs, nothing was lost. In fact, time was gained, and people got their planning decisions much more quickly.

It made sense in some ways to treat those working in the typing pool like machines. They needed some human essentials – lunch breaks, decent tea and biscuits, opportunities for advancement, pay rises, appreciation – but ultimately this was a necessity due to them being humans. They knew the deal. If they did the hours and typed fast and didn't have too many breaks, they would hit their targets and get a promotion, a pay rise and a nice bonus. Their meaning, if they got any, came from the friendships they made, the income they were able to generate and some satisfaction from the work and improving their skills over time. They may even have enjoyed listening to the voices on their headphones and learning before anyone else how a planning enquiry had panned out.

27

But, when a machine replaced them, the same job was done more quickly, with less effort and at much less cost in terms of salaries and cups of weak tea. They were, and please forgive me if I sound callous, second-rate machines.

The promise (and threat) of AI may prove to be that large chunks of what we think we're adding our 'unique human touch' to can be as effectively achieved by a machine.

Not everything, though.

Humans can empathise, they can read between the lines, and they can make authentic connections. They can create and innovate. They can have new ideas. They can care. Yes, an AI doctor might eventually be more trustworthy than a human one, but who do you want to tell you that you have cancer? When I call a call centre, is it because I want a resolution (yes), but is it also because I want someone human to hear me and to empathise with me? When I'm negotiating with my builder over the price of re-felting my shed, do I want an algorithm to generate the price (yes, for a start), or do I also want him to take pity on me and the money-pit house I bought and do me a deal out of the goodness of his heart?

If the job a human is doing benefits from their humanity, we have to stop treating them like second-rate machines.

Our humanity doesn't thrive when we are very, very busy running from one meeting to the next. It doesn't get to spread its wings when we are on call from morning to night. It doesn't remain healthy and high functioning if we are measured by two-dimensional metrics which are, often, out of our control. It doesn't grow if we are made to feel replaceable, or inadequate or taken for granted. We cannot treat people like machines if we expect them to generate clever, ground-breaking ideas, treat customers and clients with warmth and kindness or create psychologically safe environments in which diverse groups of individuals can thrive so that the business can flourish.

Being stuck with our Victorian values will be disastrous for our organisations. We will burn our best people out. We are doing it already. We will turn people off when we need them to be turned on. We will keep them so busy they can't do the job we need them to do in service of the organisation's aims. They will leave, claiming they have been offered a better salary and a better job title when, really, they were just desperate to find something that meant something and in an organisation that treated them like a thinking, feeling person.

The 'Engagement G-Spot' myth

Just think about the norms of work which are based on this belief that people must be treated like machines:

- Working hours are based on an assumption that more hours equals value added.

- Job descriptions are based on an assumption that people will complete a set of pre-determined, defined tasks and will fit, like a puzzle piece, with other people's puzzle pieces.

- Holiday leave is based on an assumption that people need a specific amount of time off per year, but not more than that.

- Sick days are based on a belief that we can rationalise a certain number of days of illness, but that time off equals loss of productivity.

- Most targets and metrics are based on a belief that we need to tell people what we want of them, and their job is to deliver that.

- Being busy/looking busy is valued because of the belief that busy equals value added.

- Highly specific processes, tick box checklists and scripted sales and customer service calls are based on the belief that people thinking for themselves is dangerous. Better to tell them exactly what to do and how to do it (the same way as you would programme a piece of tech).

- Input focus (how many calls did you make, how many emails did you answer, how many meetings did you go to?) versus outcome focus (what changed as a result of your efforts?) is based on the idea that more activity equals more impact.

- The career ladder and bonuses are based on the belief that people are two-dimensional and, if you point them at a target (eg dangle a promotion or money in front of them), they will do whatever you ask to get their reward.

- Annual appraisals are based on the belief that, if you tell people what you want them to do and to stop doing, they will do so.

- Supervision and management are based on the belief that you can direct human activity so that people spend less time thinking for themselves and more time doing what you've asked them to do, like a machine.

What else makes you feel like a machine? What does your organisation put in place to turn people into cogs?

Whenever an organisation treats people as if they are two-dimensional and will act a certain way when certain levers are pulled (like they have no mind of their own), that's evidence of the belief that people are just like machines (but not as good).

I call this the 'Engagement G-Spot myth'.

Deep down, many senior managers seem to think there is an 'Engagement G-Spot'. If they tickle their people just the right way they will be turned on by their work and do what they are told, no questions asked.

I have been asked many times how to motivate employees – what to say and how to reward the behaviour you want to see (and punish the behaviour you don't want to see). Is there a 'form of words' which will get employees excited? How do you say, 'The time for discussion is over, we've decided, now just get on with delivering the plan, please'?

I see so many leaders who believe they've listened and they've given people an opportunity to speak up, but having done so they just expect them to do the work.

What they don't recognise is that there is no 'Engagement G-Spot'. If you want engagement – by which I mean, people who want to contribute, who believe in the bigger mission and can see their part in it, who are willing to share their ideas and expertise by choice, and who will find better ways to do things because they care, who will bring their whole selves to work in service of the organisation and its bigger purpose – you can never stop the conversation because you can never get away from the fact that people are human.

Of course, when a decision is made, action must follow, but that decision is still just a decision for now. When you see how it works on the ground, it might need to be reviewed. If the context changes, you need someone to notice and speak up so that a decision that was the best answer last month doesn't become a bad decision this month. You could also go beyond that. True engagement isn't just about people keeping you informed so you can decide what to do next. True engagement is about people keeping you informed so *they* can decide what to do next. They are, after all, thinking human beings with minds of their own, not drones who report back and wait for further instruction.

If you believe they are machines, you will treat them as such, placating them to keep their humanity manageable but then demanding they put it away until next time you ask for it.

If you believe people are human, you will want them to bring that humanity to the organisation every day. You'll want them to say uncomfortable things, to point out when a situation has changed, when what you did had an unintended impact.

An organisation I worked with a few years ago had this problem. A new leadership team had come in with a new CEO. They had arrived and carried out a restructure which saw many colleagues made redundant. They also saw an opportunity for new tech to transform the business but recognised that, while people were still distrustful and hurting, they wouldn't embrace more change.

I was brought in to help heal wounds from the past and get the culture ready for more changes in the future. For more than a year we ran working sessions, training and development, offsites and surveys. I was brutally honest with the leadership team that their style was problematic for the future. They had imposed the restructuring with little consultation. When parts of that new structure clearly didn't work, they refused to alter the design. Now they were trying to impose new tech without winning back the trust they had lost and without, at a deep level, really changing their approach.

They were willing to 'try' something new (listening, consulting, distributing decision-making, getting feedback, encouraging personal growth) but hoped, eventually, that people would have had enough of the talking, would heal, stop looking backwards and be ready to embrace the future with total enthusiasm.

When people were still talking about the past a year later, the leadership team became frustrated. They said, 'We listened. We gave them an opportunity to talk about how they felt. Now we just need them to buckle in and get on board. The time for talking about this is over.'

Here's the problem. People are over it when they are over it. They get over it more quickly when they genuinely believe the changes they see in the leadership behaviours are permanent. Listening, consulting, distributing decision-making, getting feedback and encouraging personal growth don't stop. In this new world of work, you don't get to say, 'That's enough now.' The freedom to bring your whole self to your work needs to be a permanent state, built into the culture.

If people sense that the leadership team is just 'listening' so that their people will get over themselves and get back to work, their people will never truly feel they've been heard. They will never believe that their humanity is welcome. They will disengage, work-to-rule, talk about pay rises and working hours (since that's all they can influence) and you will have your beliefs reinforced – that they are just overly complex machines and that greasing the wheels with bonuses or vouchers for dinner is enough to get them back on track and doing what you've asked.

Belief 2: Most people are trying to get away with something

The second Victorian legacy which has been baked into business for so long we don't even notice it's there, is a belief that people are trying to take their employer for a ride.

Popularised by the Puritans (although predating this by many hundreds of years) was the idea that working hard would earn you a place in Heaven, while laziness would mean you were forever damned.[12] Our concepts of management and organisational structure began at around this time. As people moved from the countryside to the growing towns and cities to work in the new factories, processes were put in place to ensure people's behaviours were controlled.

They clocked in and out (so they could not lie about when they arrived and when they left). They were supervised and set targets rather than given autonomy to work at their own pace. There were car-rots (pay rises, promotions, bonuses, perks) and sticks (being called to the boss's office for a telling off, not 'getting ahead', and ultimately being fired). When we talk about a command-and-control culture, we are talking about a concept that defined the working experience of the Industrial Age.

Those at the top supervised, made the decisions, distributed the work, managed the communication and told people what to do. Those lower down did what they were told. In exchange, they were offered a degree of job security, opportunities to advance and financial reward. L David Marquet in *Leadership Is Language* calls this Redwork and Bluework.[13]

Redwork is 'doing', particularly doing 'against the clock'. It's about how much you can do in a particular amount of time, following orders, consistency and efficiency.

Bluework is the thinking. It can't be measured in units of time. In an Industrial-Age system, the Blueworkers were the leaders and managers of the Redworkers, doing all the thinking and issuing the orders. We still do this now.

Underlying that system was a whole range of beliefs which justified why it had to be this way:

- Some people are better at thinking and other people are better at doing.

- You have to earn the right to make decisions and have access to complex information. Those at the top have earned the right.

- People get to the top, to these decision-making roles, because they are better at making decisions and managing complex information than other people.

- Most people don't want to think, they just want to do a job and get paid.

- When we let everyone think for themselves, we get chaos. It's better to leave the thinking to a few people to keep things simple.

- Those with the most experience and seniority have the best ideas. The ideas from lower down the organisation tend to be poorly conceived.

- With the right information and reporting, those at the top will have the data they need to make decisions on behalf of those lower down.

- These decisions are complex and stressful. Leaders need to protect followers from information and decisions which might worry and confuse them.

- If we let people lower down the structure make decisions, they will make self-serving decisions rather than decisions that are good for the whole business.

- We have to control who has access to information, resources (like pens and stationery), influence and customers because some people will abuse the system if we don't and therefore we have to treat *everyone* like we can't trust them because of these bad apples.

Until now, one of the reasons technology has been valued so highly is because it limits the risk that people can get away with misbehaving. When you can track working hours, log expenses and have badges that give you access to certain parts of the building and not others, you can maintain control. Machines are inherently better than people because they aren't trying to get away with anything. They don't have an agenda.

When technology is introduced to an organisation with this underlying philosophy, of course people are resistant to it. They can see that technology isn't an enabler of their creativity and humanity. It is another way to control them. When humanity isn't valued, technology which reduces the need for humans in the business is rightly received with scepticism.

But when humanity is valued for what it is, technology that takes away drudgery, that sifts vast amounts of data to provide insights which humans can then feed into their creativity, and that finds ways to use the human potential of every single employee in the business in a way that is rewarding and meaningful, can finally be liberating.

If you don't understand people, you won't understand technology

Technology is often seen as replacing the need for people – 'If a machine can do it, let's get a machine to do it. Then we don't need the people. Given that the work these machines are doing is best done by a machine, it makes sense to take it away from people if you have the chance.'

But that doesn't mean we don't need people. Until now, most of our days have been filled with machine-type work – organising our diaries, organising people, answering emails, following processes, following up with people, doing research, writing reports, reading reports, analysing data, sitting in meetings while other people update our managers, filling in expenses... I could go on.

In among that we get to do some creative work, or have interesting discussions on matters of ethics, or learn something new, or connect with colleagues and clients. In a typical week, though, that's a small percentage of our time, and the work we love to do is often squeezed in around the rest of the stuff that we don't much like but is required to keep the system running.

I don't believe we've scratched the surface of what people could contribute to an organisation because we've kept them so busy doing work a machine can now do. There has never been any space for deep thinking, connecting or discussion on a day-to-day basis. We've not organised people for this kind of work because we've prioritised machine-type work. We don't even really value it as work in the same way. We value 'doing', being busy, cracking on.

But what about:

- Imagining
- Connecting with each other
- Connecting with customers and clients
- Connecting with the wider community
- Integrating the organisation with the wider world
- Connecting with themselves (deeply)
- Considering ethical topics (properly)
- Resting and recovering

- Following their sense of purpose and contribution

- Caring about others

- Having wide-ranging, rambling conversations which result in insight and enhanced awareness

- Generating ideas that take time to emerge

- Really listening

- Enjoying the process

- Collaborating with nonhuman employees to find opportunities that are missed when they are working against the clock

- Collaborating with nonhuman employees to dive deeper into topics and new ideas

- Indulging in flights of fancy which may or may not have an outcome

- Reflecting on the long-term impact of decisions

- Connecting themselves to something bigger, past and future, which informs their decisions today

We've rarely asked people to focus almost exclusively on this as their work, certainly not at the more junior levels of our organisations.

All of this untapped potential of people is sitting there, dormant. As leaders, we may not even have the skills ourselves to extract this kind of contribution from people. We're good at managing activity, not necessarily facilitating thinking. We may lack the skills to really connect with ourselves, let alone the skills to help other people do so.

But if we could, what would our organisations be capable of? If we had the machines doing what machines are first-rate at doing, and people doing what people are first-rate at doing (for the first time since the Industrial Revolution), what opportunities would we be able to generate and capitalise on? How much more innovative could our organisations be? How much more engaging and meaningful could the work be, even for junior and new employees? How much of a difference could we each make? And how much more fun would it be?

If we simply see technology as replacing the second-rate machines that people have been, we will miss this enormous potential. If you want to leave your organisation better than you found it, this seems like a great place to start.

Action 1: Create a humane environment for human beings to thrive

There's a lot of talk today about employee well-being and mental health, but the responsibility for remaining healthy, being resilient and coping with stress is typically placed on the employee.

We provide the training, coaching or counselling and then we expect people to use these tools to cope with the onslaught.

Wouldn't it be better if the causes of ill-health were addressed instead (or as well)?

What is it about the way we work that is inhumane? Consider:

- Office design and layout

- Working hours

- Meetings

- The language people use (terms like 'human resources' or 'engagement programme')

- What we ask people to do, how long we give them, the obstacles in their way

- The ways we expect people to hide their humanity, their emotions, their individuality

- The career paths available to your people

- How we promote, assign responsibility and measure people

- How we treat people day to day

- How we use time and how busy we are

What else almost inevitably creates an unhealthy environment? And whose responsibility is it to fix that?

It's too easy to blame the people in your organisation for being unable to handle everything that's expected of them, but apart from inside the Victorian factory (or perhaps a slave in ancient Egypt or equivalent), we've never worked so hard. An ancient hunter-gatherer did about 1,773 hours of work a year. In the fourteenth century, a casual labourer worked about 1,440 hours a year. The Middle Ages were a tough time and working hours went crazy in the nineteenth century, but working hours today for an average US office worker are greater than they were for a thirteenth-century peasant or even a prehistoric hunter-gatherer.[14] In addition, despite the invention of weekends and vacation time, an average medieval peasant would have only worked about 150 days of the year (what with feast days and religious festivals) compared to the average American today, who works about 244 days a year.[15] And then, of course, you've got those who do 'extreme' stints of sixty or more hours a week[16] (officially or unofficially).

As the edges of our working day blur, with many of us being connected 24/7, 365 days a year, it's for business leaders to end the madness. This is especially true when we expect our human workforce to think, create, discuss, debate, and connect with each other and with our customers. This work isn't made more effective by spending more hours at the desk. It requires people to live their lives, to get inspiration outside of their office, and take an interest in a broad range of topics. You can't carrot-and-stick creativity and innovation out of people.

Before you work on being a better leader for your people day to day, in order to bring about a future of work which actually works in the future, you'd better consider all the ways work is currently inhumane. Because, if you don't, it won't matter how much people want to do their best work, they will be unable to do so.

Start by taking out huge swathes of activity, like most meetings and expectations around working hours, working location and dress code. Given that the edges of our working day and the rest of our lives are so blurred now anyway, look for inspiration in how we live, how we gather when we aren't at work, how we speak to each other at home, how we care for each other in families (if you have a healthy one!), how other cultures care for their needy, how other cultures create a sense of belonging and community.

Be inspired by history, by sci-fi, by spiritual and religious concepts... in fact, by anything that isn't the twentieth and twenty-first-century office. Then start bug-fixing. There are no right answers here. No one has yet created a utopian working environment. Try something – something radical if you wish – and then learn from the experience, refine and go again. Just remain as humane and kind as you can throughout the process.

LISTEN NOW

To understand more about the potential, and threat, of AI, I wanted to talk to Jordi Ferrer. As head of ServiceNow's UK and Ireland business (www. servicenow.com), he knows first-hand what this new technology is capable of.

You can listen to the interview at **www. buzzsprout.com/2250059/13633422**, or listen

to any of the other interviews here: **https://
punksinsuitshowtoleadtheworkplacereformation.
buzzsprout.com**

Summary

The world is being disrupted by new technology. Business and the way we work need disruption too. We need to think about this new technology as a 'nonhuman workforce' to differentiate it from the human workforce. Our old Industrial-Age hardwiring about people as second-rate machines who are always trying to get away with something means we have undervalued their humanity and tried, as far as possible, to replace them with machines or treat them like machines.

Today we need their humanity, but there is no 'Engagement G-Spot'. Instead, we need to create a humane working environment.

As a leader, your job is to disrupt the status quo to bring about change.

Questions to consider

- Where are the tensions in my everyday work?

- Who else could I ask about this? Who else might notice or experience tensions in the system?

- Who benefits from it being done this way? (Or who could I ask about this?)

- What do we tell ourselves is the justification for doing it this way? How does that justification reinforce Victorian beliefs about people?

- If I rejected those Victorian beliefs, would this system, process or activity be needed?

- If we didn't waste our time on such systems, processes or activities, what could we more usefully do instead?

- What am I picturing (even if it's unclear) in future?

- Who else could I involve in this questioning?

- What could I do about this right now?

Trust
Anarchy In The Workplace

Every January, a report called 'The Edelman Trust Barometer' comes out describing the state of global trust in major institutions including governments, NGOs, the media and businesses.[17] The results are always sobering.

Launched in 2000, the report charts how trust has changed, influenced by trends like globalisation, the Iraq War, the recession of 2008, and the rise of social media and automation.

I suggest checking it out when it's published (January of every year with updates throughout the year) but there are a few highlights to note:[18]

1. There are massive inequalities in trust. To quote their summary of twenty years of the report, 'The fortunate few have far higher levels of trust

in the system than the many. And the gap is getting wider.'

2. NGOs used to be the most trusted institution. Now it's business – but only just. Governments, media and NGOs are considered either unethical, incompetent or both. CEOs are considered more trustworthy than government leaders.

3. We don't trust sources of information. The rise in 'fake news' means people don't know which sources of information are reliable.

4. People are increasingly fearful of 'the system'. The 2017 report found that more than half of people felt the system – the networks of social living on which they depend for health, wealth and happiness – was failing them.

5. Automation, the pace of change, the huge profits made by some companies, globalisation, incompetent governments, a perception that NGOs and organisations like the UN don't do what they promise, distrust in the media as a source of information and a sense that they will be less well-off in five years than they are now, all feed these fears. Our society is perceived as unfair.

You can dig in to find out the data for your own country. At a recent speaking event in Sweden, I was challenged by an audience member who felt that the Nordic countries were unlikely to follow this trend being, by nature, less hierarchical and fairer than other parts of the world. Not so. In fact, according to the 2023 report, Sweden is in the 'severely polarised' category along with Spain, South Africa, Argentina, Colombia and the US.[19] Brazil, France, the UK, Japan, Italy, Mexico, South Korea, the Netherlands and Germany are in the 'in danger of severe polarisation' category.

This is important. We may perceive trust rather differently from other people in our country or organisation, particularly those lower down the hierarchy, from different backgrounds or a different gender. It might look much rosier to some than to others.

It's clear we have a problem, globally. Our customers (whether they are private individuals or employees of other companies) and the people who work for us are impacted by changing values, by global events, by shifts in prevailing attitudes, by emerging sensitivities and a growing awareness of particular issues. Whether it's climate change and the existential crisis which bothers many of us, whether it's longer working lives and the prospect of still being in paid employment in our seventies or beyond, whether it's new technologies which threaten our jobs or whether it's the latest politician's faux pas relentlessly hitting our Facebook feed, we are all vulnerable to the changes in our world.

How we feel on any particular day is based not only on how well we slept or how our children talked to us that morning, but on bigger trends – whether they be threats or opportunities – which are changing our experience of living on this planet.

Distrust in our leaders leads to 'moral distress', where we feel unable to live in a way that's true to our values and ethics. Distrust in the 'other' means we struggle to embrace diversity or seek out healthy conflict. Distrust in technology means we will fear new developments or miss opportunities to shape that technology. Distrust in the system may mean we don't vote, don't campaign for issues that are important to us, don't stand up for our rights or don't believe things can ever get better, so what's the point in trying?

In organisations, distrust leads to a variety of behaviours, by managers and by individual contributors which limit the potential of the organisation and its people.

Controlling systems and processes

In Chapter 1, I outlined two Victorian beliefs which still underpin how we see people in an organisation – *People are second-rate machines* and *People are always trying to get away with something*.

These beliefs date from the Industrial Age when we had a relatively stable society in which people had respect for their elders, their betters, the boss, community leaders and the press. Hierarchies were built into the fabric of society. In the UK, we had (and still have) a royalty, a landed class, a middle class, a working class and 'the poor and wretched'. I'm oversimplifying. Our class system was and remains complex, but back then you doffed your cap to the Lord and Lady of the Manor, and you called your boss 'Mr Jones' or even 'Sir', not 'Steve'. The key to the executive bathroom and dining room were acceptable perks for those at the top.

But the systems that produced compliance, predictability and efficiency won't work today.

People's expectations of work have changed. We are moving up Maslow's hierarchy of needs. Today we seek self-actualisation. We want to express who we are. Self-actualised people don't want to be told what to do. They want to partner, to collaborate, to co-create. They expect to do work that makes a difference.

Nine out of ten employees would be willing to swap a percentage of their lifetime earnings for more meaningful work.[20] Fifty-six per cent of workers won't even consider a job at a company that has values they disagree with.[21] Eighty-four per cent of workers who worked from home during the pandemic said they plan to carry on some form of hybrid working in the future.[22]

This isn't about bending over backwards to satisfy unrealistic demands from workers who want it all. It's about the nature of the work we are asking them to do and how we get the best from them. Even if you don't really care if your employees find their work meaningful for any altruistic reason, there is a clear business imperative to change the nature of work, driven not only by what employees expect but by what your organisation expects of them.

In the Industrial Age, the structures and rules of the organisation chimed with the needs and expectations of the workforce. They wanted safety and security, respect and status. The organisation wanted efficiency, predictability and compliance. That system worked because there was alignment. Factory owners may not have genuinely cared that their workers had a nicer car to show off to their friends, but they recognised that dangling a company car would result in a productivity benefit. The cost of the car was by far outweighed by the financial benefit to the business. Everyone won. These days, though, the company car isn't enough.

When today's employees find their work meaningful, companies save an average of $6.43 million in annual turnover-related costs for every 10,000 workers.[23] Productivity improves by up to 33%,[24] worth around $10,000 per employee.[25] So even if you don't care that your employees find their work meaningful, what do you have to lose by making it so? Not only do you lose nothing, but you stand to gain a huge productivity benefit and a reduction in costs.

What's trust got to do, got to do with it?

The foundation of creating meaningful work is trust. Your business might be purpose-led. You may contribute a percentage of your profits to good causes. You may be part of a working group advocating for better living conditions for people in your community. You might volunteer at the local food bank.

But if your people don't trust you, none of that will matter.

The absence of trust is Patrick Lencioni's number one dysfunction of a team.[26] Without trust, there cannot be psychological safety, and without that, there cannot be healthy conflict. Healthy conflict leads to great ideas and solutions. When people don't feel they can highlight tensions in the system, problems, the unintended consequences of well-meaning decisions, opportunities which challenge the status quo and differences of perspective which enrich the thinking, great decisions can't occur. Without healthy conflict, tensions between people fester. People give up trying to make things better and just complain, quietly, about how things are. People may seek to find meaning in their work despite the prevailing culture but, certainly, the culture is a barrier to that rather than an enabler.

Difficult environments which inhibit people from making a difference, seeing the impact of their work or working in partnership with others, undermine engagement. Poorly thought-through decisions, decisions which don't stick, decisions which don't result in action or in actions which don't achieve their intended results are bad for business. It's pretty obvious.

But when companies see evidence of bad decisions, what do the leaders tend to do? They shift back into their Victorian hardwiring which says, 'People are trying to get away with something.' They assume stupidity, lack of capability, nefarious intent, personal agendas or laziness. They take back responsibility. They say, 'Other people don't know how to solve problems. Only I can solve problems properly. I tried empowering but now I can see these people can't make good choices. I will just have to make their decisions for them.'

When they see tensions between people, they revert to their Victorian hardwiring which says, 'People are second-rate machines. If only people would just put their differences aside and get on with the job. That's what we pay them for. I will step in, fix this and then people can get on with what they are meant to be doing.'

But the cause of poor decisions, personal tensions and a propensity for leaders to step back in and 'fix things' has its roots in low trust.

The two elements of trust

Trust has two elements – being trustworthy and being willing to trust. Let's explore them now.

Being trustworthy

As we've seen, as a planet, we have lost our trust in authority figures. We don't trust politicians, the media, NGOs or business leaders as a breed, and with good reason. People turn up or log in of a morning already not trusting authority. What makes you any different?

What is different is proximity. The '2023 Edelman Trust Barometer' says that we are most likely to trust our colleagues, friends, neighbours and our CEO as sources of information.[27] Why? Because they are real human beings to us. We can see the whites of their eyes.

While we may not be in the same physical space daily with our work colleagues due to the rise of hybrid working, we do have regular interactions or know their reputation from people we trust.

Your number one job as a leader now is to *be worthy of trust.*

That means knowing what you stand for, and standing for it, and creating authentic human connections (or Intimacy) with others.

I get a flavour of what a company's culture is like by the way they treat me as an external consultant. Do they ghost me for months and suddenly reappear, hugely enthusiastic and expecting me to be ready with a proposal by the end of play tomorrow? What about if I've pitched for a project and they never follow up? Do they pay on time and how simple (or complex) is the process of getting paid? How many hoops do I have to jump through?

Don't get me wrong. I'm a big girl and am rarely unsettled. I have been in business for twenty-five years and can take the rough and tumble. What I find informative and useful about these experiences is that they are almost always indicative of a systemic, probably cultural, issue in the organisation.

Many organisations claim to care about people – employees, customers and suppliers – but the real test of whether they care is in how they treat people they don't need. If a company decides not to work with me, for instance, they don't need me. In that situation, do they stay true to their stated values and provide timely decisions and honest feedback? Doing that might be awkward and time-consuming. Maybe they only stay true to their values when it's worth it to them.

If I don't get a timely response and some feedback, what about their junior employees? What about people in the organisation who speak up and call out unacceptable behaviours? What about people who challenge the status quo or point out systemic failures? What about exiting employees or people on short-term contracts? What about small customers who don't add as much to the bottom line as bigger customers?

Knowing what you stand for and standing for it applies at a personal level and at an organisational level – and it's hard. There is often a cost to staying true to what you believe. If you say people are your greatest asset, you have to recognise what that means when you're having a bad year. If you say you care about the environment, you have to face up to the ways your business harms the environment, even if it's costly to fix. When you're in a meeting and you don't like a decision that seems inevitable, you have to say something about it. Maybe other people will be uncomfortable. Maybe they will resent you for putting a spanner in the works. Maybe they'll be annoyed that you've delayed their lunch break with your objections.

But if you claimed that something mattered to you, and then in the meeting you weren't willing to put it on the table, how can you expect people to trust you?

I'm not saying you have to be obnoxious or put your job on the line for every opinion you have. I'm not saying you have to lay down an ultimatum. You can use your emotional intelligence to pick your moment and the context for speaking your truth. In the end, you may be over-ruled. You win some, you lose some.

But if you aren't going to follow up your words with your deeds then don't be surprised if people don't trust you and if they think, 'They are just like the rest – not to be trusted.'

Just to be clear, if your values are 'profit first, people second', you go for it! There are far too many organisations claiming that kindness, authenticity, integrity and quality are their values (what I described as 'Bland Values' in my last book[28]) when, in truth, their values are shareholder return, ambition, winning and cashing out at the first opportunity. It's not for me to tell you what should matter to you. We need all types of business. Business can be a force for good in the world (I have a whole chapter on it), but that might not be your priority. You don't have to have high-and-mighty values.

Knowing what you stand for and standing for it still applies. Pretending people are your number one asset when, in fact, share price is your primary metric, creates distrust. Far better to shout it loud and proud: 'We stand for making lots and lots of money, whatever the cost to our employees' well-being.' You will find your tribe. You will attract employees who want to be part of that and who share your love of the dollar.

Now, if this applies to you, I have to tell you that there is a lot in this book that you're not going to like. I've given you fair warning. At the same time, I admire your chutzpa and encourage you to own it. At least people will know what they are getting. Your words and deeds will align and they will appreciate knowing where they stand. Far better that than to constantly undermine trust by pretending you have a set of values that you have no intention of upholding.

In addition to knowing what you stand for and standing for it, is what I call 'Intimacy'. This is a willingness to reveal who you are 'under the suit'. Maybe you don't wear a suit. Most people seem not to today. Regardless, we have low trust in authority figures, and we no longer trust the gloss and polish. Any sense that you are hiding your true colours will be sniffed out by other people.

Authentic human connection is the difference between pretending to care and caring. There's a famous misquote, attributed to Dwight D Eisenhower: 'Leadership is the art of getting someone to do what you want him to do but think it was his idea.' The actual quote is 'Leadership is the art of getting someone else to do something you want done because he wants to do it', which is slightly less manipulative but has at its heart the idea that leaders have the brilliant idea and then get buy-in from others who realise how brilliant the idea is and that they want it too.

It's no surprise that the misquote is the one most people repeat because it speaks to our deep-rooted belief that the leader knows what is best for others.

The job of leadership is to work out what is right and then use whatever techniques they have to show other people the right way. You could force them, of course, using your authority as the boss, to get them to do what you want. But working life is more pleasant if you can convince them that it's in their best interest to do what you want. When they finally 'get it', you can move forward together.

This has been the thinking behind the vast majority of transformation programmes, re-structures, culture-change programmes and company mergers.

The people at the top have the idea. Perhaps, if they are more enlightened, they seek ideas and opinions from the rest of the organisation. This is overwhelming since everyone wants something different, so they end up making the decision they would have made even without the consultation. At least they know what the objections are going to be so they can prepare their communications to explain why decisions were made, why not everyone got their way and why, in the end, this is the right thing to do.

Then the plan is put in place and rolled out. Any resistance is put down to poor communication ('Let's explain again so they understand "The Why"') or the inadequacy of individuals to embrace change. Companies tend to avoid talking about Tell and Sell these days as it feels dictatorial, but whatever you call it, most organisations do a lightly disguised version of it.

In contrast, authentic human connection is about recognising that you, the leader, are human like everyone else. You have an opinion, you have experience and expertise, but you are also flawed. You don't know the right thing to do. You don't have all the answers. You have days of struggling with imposter syndrome.

Good news. You no longer have to act like you are superhuman. Authentic human connection means tapping into your values and *being* those values at work. It means being open about what you are struggling with, what matters to you, what you are unsure about and what you are looking for from others. It means recognising that you, and a bunch of other human beings, are going to bring your humanity to solving problems.

When you hide behind your metaphorical suit, when you put on a mask and present a polished version of yourself to others, a shell which keeps your soft insides protected, it is impossible for others to break through. They feel disconnected. They know they are not getting the real you. They wonder what you are hiding. What is your real motive? What is really going on?

As a result, they keep themselves shut off too, hiding behind their own shell, and putting on their own mask. Now you are isolated. You wonder, 'What do they really think? What are they struggling with? What aren't they telling me?'

Now you have mutual distrust.

I'm not suggesting you have to bring your worst self to work every day. We have many versions of ourselves and we are entitled to flex between them. Who I am when I'm with my daughter is different to who I am when I'm on stage. It's all still me, just different flavours of me for different purposes.

But to make authentic connections you have to be curious about others, to reject the notion that you are stronger, better, wiser and more capable than others. You have to be willing to connect with your emotions, not just your logical brain.* If you are not connected with yourself you can't connect with others.

This is something we are rarely taught. When I ask someone how they are they reply 'Fine'. Maybe they reply 'Busy'. When I ask people to explain how they are, they often explain what they are thinking eg 'I feel that no one is listening to me', or, 'I feel like my manager has another agenda'. These aren't feelings. They are thoughts.

A feeling would be 'I feel depleted', 'I feel worried' or 'I feel discouraged'. Or 'I feel optimistic', 'I feel calm', 'I feel humbled'. Most likely, they feel mixed emotions – worried and optimistic with a smattering of depleted.

Beyond that, feelings can be physical sensations. Sometimes when I am coaching a client, I have a physical sensation in response to what they are saying and cannot articulate the emotion, only my body's response. I might feel tightness in my chest, bubbles in my stomach or heat from my forehead, and I will tell clients about it. I will say, 'When you said that, I felt my chest tighten. What happened to you when you said that?' I don't necessarily convey meaning from that sensation. I am aware that my reaction is

---

* Have a look at this list of feelings and consider which ones you are feeling now: www.hoffmaninstitute.org/wp-content/uploads/Practices-FeelingsSensations.pdf, accessed 1 December 2023

mine. I might feel tightness because I wouldn't want to be in the situation they are in. That doesn't mean they feel the same. It's a trigger for a question rather than evidence of anything. I don't know them better than they know themselves.

Knowing what you stand for (and standing for it) and making authentic human connections (Intimacy) create trust. People are more likely to trust someone they know and someone who is consistent in their words and actions. They may be cynical at the start, testing you to see if you mean what you say, but over time they will come to see that you are worthy of trust.

When they trust you, they will be more likely to open up to you, to trust you with their truth. This is how you will learn more about what's really going on, what people really think, the barriers they are facing and what you can do to help them.

You won't have to 'sell' them on your idea and 'convince' them that they want it too. Your perspective will be shaped by what you learn. They will develop their own answers (we will come back to this), and having developed their own answers, they will be inspired to take action and move things forward. That ownership and sense of responsibility that you've been trying to convince them to take will happen without you needing to Tell and Sell.

This is a huge shift from the Victorian-Age approach. Not only are you treating others as people, not second-rate machines, but you get to be a person too. This is one of the ways we must go back to a more ancient way of working. When we think about human evolution, we really haven't evolved in the last few hundred years, and yet the way we live and work has changed enormously. We aren't suited to sitting at a desk, working 9–9, eating lunch at our desks (at home or in an office), chugging tea and coffee all day to sustain ourselves, putting on a mask to appear 'professional'. No wonder so many people struggle with stress, ill-health brought on by work, and even burn-out. No wonder petty battles and politics play such a large part in how we work and how we need to be to survive work.

None of that contributes to the success of the business. Even if your primary motive is to make huge profits which boost the company's share price, anything which detracts from this, like squabbles between teams or the poor mental health of your people, will be a concern to you. If you believe that your business is potentially a force for good in the world, this is even more true. How can you say, on the one hand, 'We are here to make the world a better place', and on the other say, 'We will have to break our people in order to make that happen'?

Being worthy of trust is much more than transparent communication. It is a far deeper shift to authenticity, connection and values. As a leader, that shift starts with you before you can expect anyone else to do the same.

Willingness to trust

Being willing to trust is the second element of creating trust. When I started speaking to audiences about trust, I talked about how to become trustworthy. It was a different time. Today, your willingness to trust others is, if anything, more important.

This is partly because your willingness to trust others has a direct influence on their willingness to trust you. How can you expect them to hand you their trust when you are unwilling to do the same?

Sometimes, after a speech, an audience member will come up to me and tell me that they agree with everything I said. They will add that they are pleased that so-and-so particular person heard it too because they need to change!

Here's what I think when I'm told that – 'You've been thinking about what everyone else needs to do differently, not what you need to do differently.' The problem with that is we cannot make others change. We might be able to give feedback and that feedback might go in, but it's easy to see all the things other people must do. It's much harder to look inside ourselves and ask, 'What is the part I play in perpetuating this issue?' That's the only element we have total control over – our own attitudes and behaviours. We think others should go through the discomfort of change but we are not willing to go through the discomfort of change ourselves.

There are myriad ways we put limits on our willingness to trust. We say we trust, but we step in and make decisions for others. We say we trust, but we want to see all expenses claims over £100. We say we trust, but we want final sign-off of anything that's going to senior management. We say we trust, but we arrange constant update meetings so we can see exactly what is going on at all times.

What if you trusted? What if you believed people weren't trying to get away with anything? What if you believed the people you worked with cared as much as you about doing a good job?

That would mean that, if someone made a mistake, your assumption wouldn't be 'What an idiot, give that to me.' It would be curiosity. What information was unavailable to them that would have been valuable? What support could I have offered (without doing the job for them) to help them get it right? What did they learn about the barriers they encountered which will enable them to get a better outcome next time? What stopped them from seeking my input? Do they trust me?

When Ricardo Semler was CEO of Semco, a Brazilian business well-known, in part, because it has almost no rules, he began questioning everything. His father had a more conventional style of leadership, but when Ricardo took over he began to ask some questions. Why do we need an office? Isn't that just our ego? Why do we interview people the way we do? Shouldn't they check us out before believing our hype about ourselves? Why shouldn't people set their own salaries? He describes this as 'looking for wisdom' and it is based on a fundamental belief that people can be trusted.[29]

Early on, some employees took advantage of these freedoms – stealing tools and keeping them at home for instance – but when they realised that they could take tools when they needed them without being frisked at the door, as happened in Semler's father's day, and simply return them and borrow them again if and when they needed them, no questions asked, there was no reason to steal.

Take a look at the limits you put on your willingness to trust. Those are the limits people put on their willingness to trust you. Find ways to extend those limits until trust is baked into your culture.

Leader is trusted	Charismatic leader-follower	Safe, collaborative, innovative learning culture
Leader isn't trusted	Command and control	Leader lacks credibility, is unsafe
	Leader doesn't trust others	Leader trusts others

Leadership/Trust model

It can be difficult to figure out whether you have a trust problem because issues with trust don't present as issues with trust. People don't walk around telling you they don't trust you, and you may believe you do trust them. The Leadership/Trust model aims to help you work out whether you have a trust problem and, if so, what kind.

Charismatic leader-follower

In the Industrial Age, the leader was superior. They were trusted. It was assumed they knew what they were doing. They had the years of experience and the accoutrements (the car, the handmade suit, the watch, the education, the nice house). They were the 'answers person'. They knew everything and everyone. They had access to information you didn't have and they made decisions for you. You did what they said.

This is the charismatic leader-follower model. In my early days as a coach, I would ask clients to name some leaders, past or present, so we could discuss their qualities and what made them leaders. Can you guess who always came up? Winston Churchill, Margaret Thatcher, Hitler, Steve Jobs, Mother Teresa. Without fail. Love them or loathe them, these are perfect examples of charismatic leader-follower types. We admire or fear them. They can generate huge, unquestioning followership – an almost religious loyalty.

With perhaps the exception of Mother Teresa, they aren't known for being great listeners. It wasn't important that they trusted others, distributed decision-making, remained curious about new perspectives, took off the mask and revealed who they were. They were leaders because of their position and their position made them leaders.

This is what happens when you are in the top-left box: blind followership. You'll know if you're here because:

- People will defer decisions to you

- They will ask for permission

- They will go through you rather than talk directly to others

- They will doubt their ability

- They will not take the initiative – you will have to instruct

- They will believe you are superior to them

- They will feel a little afraid of you

- They won't know much about you and your life

- They won't tell you much about theirs

- They will tell you what you want to hear

- They will take your side against others

- They will never question your thinking

- They won't give you feedback

- They will go over and above to please you

- They act like your children and you are their parent

- They will seek to be around you, in proximity to your power

Have you experienced any of this? When you think about people who behave this way around you, how do you collude with or perpetuate this perspective of you? Do you rather like it? Is your ego fed by it? Do you believe that some people just need this from you because it's their nature? Are you trying to break the habit but don't know how?

The key here is to examine the limits of your willingness to trust others. Think about when you step in to solve problems that others should sit with themselves. Think about how you protect people from being uncomfortable and take on that discomfort yourself. Think about the processes and systems (the reports you ask for to keep you updated, the numerous meetings that you chair, the decisions you hold on to) that reinforce that they are not to be trusted. How do you deal with mistakes? Do you fix, rescue, take back responsibility or even get angry?

You demonstrate that you don't trust in myriad subtle ways, and, because you don't trust them, they don't trust themselves. As a result, they continue to defer to you, oh wise one. In addition, over time, they find less and less reward in their work. They may start to see the cracks you've been trying to keep hidden. They start to wonder whether you really are as all-powerful as they thought and they start to lose trust in you. You will inevitably get something wrong. You are only human. Now they are disillusioned. You loved being the hero or heroine but now it's come back to bite you.

Command and control

When you don't trust people and people don't trust you, you have to rely on command-and-control leadership to get anything done. You lean on threats and rewards, carrot and stick.

You have to be the 'answers person' and, regardless of whether people trust your answers, they are forced to comply because you're the boss. Instead of being inspired and motivated by a sense of meaning and purpose, they are motivated by not getting fired or by getting (or missing) a bonus at the end of the year. They move down Maslow's hierarchy of needs. In lieu of the freedom to influence anything but their salary and job title, they become obsessed with salary and job title.

You will know if you are in the bottom-left box because:

- You have to do all the thinking

- People are constantly asking you what to do next

- People are highly resistant to change and need inducements

- You have a high turnover of staff

- You have low morale in the team

- People behave like naughty children

- No one takes the initiative

- People work-to-rule

- People take advantage (proving your deep-down belief that people are always trying to get away with something)

- You have lots of processes and systems to ensure people do things 'the right way'

- You don't have any time

- You are focused on today's crisis

- You work harder than anyone else

The shift here starts with trusting others. Don't start by trying to get others to trust you. How can you expect them to do something you aren't willing to do? Besides, they've learnt not to trust you because of the way you've behaved until now. They can't just switch trust back on.

Start by treating them like you trust them. This is an important distinction. Right now, you don't trust them. No one can force you to trust, and you have no reason to believe they can be trusted, yet, but you can *treat people like you trust them.*

You can ask yourself, 'If I did trust them, what would I do now?', 'If I did trust them, how would I get out of their way?', or, 'If I did trust them what would my role be?'

In time, once they start to see that you trust them, you can demonstrate the ways you are worthy of their trust. They will be more open to seeing you as a human, making authentic human connections with you, and recognising the ways you stand for what you believe. Of course, don't delay doing this second part! Start now. I'm just warning you that you'll have to show you trust them before they will notice how hard you've been working to prove you are worthy of their trust.

Leader lacks credibility, is unsafe

You may trust your people, but they don't trust you. As I explained above, this might be a phase as you show a willingness to trust them but haven't quite earned their trust in return.

Equally, it might be because you genuinely lack credibility in their eyes. This can happen when you feel the need to be 'one of the gang'. Instead of embracing true leadership, you undermine yourself and your capabilities. You use self-deprecating language about yourself, you don't speak up in meetings when senior people are present, you say something is important to you but you don't stand for it and you reveal too much about yourself and your flaws without balancing that with your strengths and areas of competence. You are unpredictable, sometimes assured, sometimes listening deeply, and other times dismissive or reverting to command and control. People don't know where they stand with you.

This creates an unsafe environment. No one knows which version of you they are going to meet, or they don't believe you know what you're doing. They don't trust what you say because you don't stand up for your principles and they don't believe you'll stand up for them (or stand up *to* them) if required.

You'll know if you don't have their trust (even if you trust them) because:

- They will bypass you to get to more authoritative people

- They will be resistant to your coaching and mentoring, preferring you stay out of their way

- They won't take on board your feedback

- They will cancel 1-2-1 time with you

- They will agree to decisions you make in the moment but not act on them

- They will tell you everything is fine when it isn't

- They will say you're very nice but...

- You will see them modeling your behaviour by not speaking up to people they consider more powerful, not collaborating, not encouraging healthy debate or input from elsewhere in the organisation

- Your team may be isolated and not included in decisions that should include your perspective

- Others at your level will be getting ahead but you won't

- Your manager will be giving you low-level projects and not challenging you with new problems to address

- When you speak, no one listens, although when someone else says the same thing it's taken seriously

Your job, if this isn't just a phase you're going through, is to work on your self-esteem. Self-esteem and self-confidence are different things. Self-confidence is a belief you can do a particular activity. You may lack confidence because you've never tried something before, but once you've had more experience your confidence grows. Self-esteem is the belief that you are capable and worthy. If you lack self-esteem you will never feel good enough even if you have confidence in your skill. People with high self-esteem are willing to take risks, to put themselves out of their comfort zone and grow because they trust themselves to survive that process. People with low self-esteem avoid situations that might reinforce their belief that they aren't good enough.

Self-deprecating humour has its place. If your authority is *too* high with a particular audience (top-left box), humour can show others you are human too. Take it too far, though, and you lose credibility. Given that leadership is in the eye of the beholder, the only authority you have is that given to you by others. People don't have to see you as a leader. You have to earn their trust.

Focus on your strengths, get support and input where you have blind spots. Revel in your innate qualities and add value to your organisation by bringing those strengths to interactions and solving problems. Get used to stepping away from the detail and taking more of a leadership perspective, and be willing to let go of the types of work you did when you were new to the industry. Find out the unique ways you add value and double down on those.

Safe, collaborating, innovative learning culture
This is where you need to be. Others trust you and you trust others. You are constantly assessing your willingness to trust and taking action to give more. When you notice that you or a process is getting in the way, you get it or yourself out of the way.

You will know you are here because:

- People are willing to speak their truth

- There is a vibrancy to discussions where people play devil's advocate and invite different perspectives to the room

- People feel they have the right to seek input from elsewhere, to collaborate across teams and functions and levels of seniority

- They tell you when something is going wrong, not so you can fix it but because they value your perspective to enhance their own

- People tell you their ideas and challenge yours

- People give you helpful feedback

- People are curious, they want to grow and they don't mind getting something wrong or asking a naïve question

- People know where they stand with you and what you stand for

- You bring your unique lens to discussions even if that means you see things differently to someone else (including authority figures)

- Your views evolve and you are willing to let go of perspectives that no longer sit right with you, even if you strongly advocated for them in the past

- You are transparent about the journey you're on, which gives people permission to be transparent about where they are in their journey and what they are struggling with

- You openly acknowledge what is hard for you

Above all, you recognise that staying in this top-right box requires constant attention. Have you become complacent? Are you still as honest as you were or have you found a comfortable place with people and don't want to agitate things? Are you learning? Are you busy or do you have time to think? Has hierarchy crept in, or do you feel like an equal with your colleagues but with different roles? Are you getting drawn into detail or are you inhabiting a leadership perspective more of the time?

Action 2: Where do you put limits on your willingness to trust?

In Chapter 1, we saw that creating a humane environment was the first action to take to shift away from Victorian beliefs about people in a world where technology is transforming how we work and live, leaving space for people's humanity to be their primary asset.

You won't do this if there are limits on your willingness to trust others. If you believe, fundamentally, that people cannot be trusted and that chaos will ensue if you treat people like they are trusted, then you will keep tight controls in place, just in case you are proven correct.

There is something very appealing about distrusting others, or withholding trust until people prove they are worthy of it. It feeds our ego. We operate from a mindset that says, 'I am better than them.' We believe in our ability to do hard things, handle hard truths, make decisions and live with the consequences, but we don't believe others can do the same.

One reason why we are stuck with an outdated attitude towards people and their contribution to our organisations is that leaders have not wanted to admit they are no better than anyone else. What is the special value you bring if you are no better than the people who work for you? And, if you're no better than anyone else, why did you bother working so hard to get to where you are today? What is the prize?

If the prize is that decisions sit with you, you get to overrule others and you get access to information that isn't widely known, you are operating from the same mindset as someone from the 1960s who was obsessed with getting the keys to the executive bathroom. It means you are deriving your worth from your status.

But in this new world of work, where we have to access the humanity of the people in our organisations to solve complex challenges against a backdrop of constant uncertainty, you have to be braver. You have to let go of the accoutrements of power, the ego-boosters, and the superiority complex, and enable the wisdom of every single person in your organisation. You might be smart, but you aren't smarter than all of them.

That requires you to constantly question the limits of your willingness to trust and look for the systemic ways your organisation limits trust. Look at how decisions are made, how information is withheld and how people are monitored and supervised. Listen out for conversations where the intent is to 'protect' people from decisions and information they probably can't handle. Listen out for the implication that people will take advantage of particular freedoms or will revert to their innate laziness. Do you notice fears around anarchy, chaos and dissent unless people are closely managed? How are people tracked and measured?

And then ask, 'What would we do if we trusted people? What if people wanted to do a good job here? How would we proceed then?'

LISTEN NOW

David L Marquet is a former US nuclear submarine captain and bestselling author of *Turn the Ship Around* and *Leadership Is Language*. I quote him throughout this book as he has extraordinary personal experience of the power of making some of the changes I describe. He rethought his leadership style and passed his authority down to his crew because he felt deeply that one brain (his) could not be as intelligent as all the brains on board combined.

In our conversation, we discuss trust and what it means, the difference between Redwork and Bluework, and he even gives a sneak peek into what he's writing about next. During the interview, David shows me an old photo of a foreman in a factory and he talks through what the image shows and what it represents, so you'll hear him refer to that.

You can listen to the interview at **www. buzzsprout.com/2250059/13663386**, or listen to any of the other interviews here: **https:// punksinsuitshowtoleadtheworkplacereformation. buzzsprout.com**

Summary

We live at a time when trust in authority figures and institutions is low. It's not always personal, but people won't automatically trust you. Without two-way trust, it will be harder to get engagement, innovation, collaboration, healthy debate and good decisions. You will have to revert to an authoritative style of leadership which destroys motivation and denies people the right to get meaning from their work. It also makes your job less meaningful and keeps you stuck issuing orders.

Becoming trustworthy entails knowing what you stand for and standing for it, and building authentic human connections (Intimacy) with others.

Both of these require you to understand your true values and be transparent and consistent about what these are.

Being willing to trust entails examining the subtle limits you put on your willingness to trust others.

Questions to consider

- What do I stand for? What are my values?

- When do I shy away from bringing those values to the table? What stops me?

- Where am I inconsistent? Do I apply a set of values to one group of people but not another? Do I sometimes stand for what I believe and other times not?

- Do people know what matters to me and what my values and guiding principles are?

- Have I invested in getting to know people? Do they know me?

- What do I keep hidden? What if I brought that to my work and relationships at work?

- What am I feeling? Can I put names to the emotions?

- How can I stay more connected with my emotions and the feelings in my body, and what value would that add to my leadership?

- What are the limits I put on my willingness to trust others?

- What systems and processes give people the impression they aren't trusted?

- If I trusted others, what would I stop doing? What would I start doing? What would we do differently as an organisation?

- How do I get in the way of people doing their jobs? How do I get in the way of people's growth? How do I get in the way of people's deeper connection with their meaning and purpose?

- What am I going to do differently now?

CHAPTER 3

HIERARCHY

Hierarchy
Stairway To The Boardroom

C ommand and control structures are built into our organisations by the hierarchies we have established.

No matter how much we might claim we want to empower people, we want people to step up, we want people to challenge authority, or we want people to take ownership and initiative, the hierarchy is proof that we don't mean it.

Even if you take layers out of your organisation, the hierarchy often persists. We have had 250 years of organisational hierarchies. Even our education system was constructed to teach children early how a hierarchy works and how to operate within that structure.

Hierarchical hardwiring leads to compliance, moderation, gameplay, politics, a slow pace of change, parent-child behaviour, lack of engagement, favouritism, siloes, selfishness, feelings of exclusion, duplication of effort, busy-work, a lack of accountability, diminished returns on investment per hour, presenteeism and a power gradient.

That's because, at its heart, lie the two Victorian beliefs I've talked about already. Hierarchy is the embodiment of a machine mindset, which treats people like cogs in that machine and puts in place structures and processes to make them behave in a machine-like manner. Or, at least, that is the intention. Of course, people are not machines which is why they don't just comply but start finding ways to game the system, to exert some kind of influence over the constraints in their path and normalise workarounds. We will explore this further in this chapter.

Let's be clear – there is no 'correct' organisational structure. Whichever way you organise people and work there will be upsides and downsides. We are not going to explore different organisational structure models here for this reason. When it comes to totally dismantling hierarchy and replacing it with self-managing, nonhierarchical organisational structures, there are better books than this which provide a how-to guide.[30, 31]

Nevertheless, understanding how hierarchy, perceptions of hierarchy and hierarchical hardwiring limit the capabilities of your people at a time when you need to liberate all of their capabilities, will help you see the part you play in perpetuating it. Perhaps you will go self-managing. Perhaps you'll be the one to initiate that transformation. Perhaps you can see an alternative structure that reduces some of the tensions currently existing in the organisation. But unless you do something about the *emotional* hardwiring and the *behaviours* which reinforce the power structure within your organisation every day, it won't matter how many layers you take out or where you rearrange the chairs, people will continue to seek out the powerful players and wield their power in myriad ways.

Cogs and wheels

The organisational hierarchy is another Victorian invention. Of course, there were hierarchies in the military and the church going back hundreds (thousands) of years, but the first organisational chart[32] dates from 1855 and is attributed to a Scottish-born engineer called Daniel McCallum (a beautiful, flower-like expression of how duties were assigned in the New York and Erie Railroad), which was intended to clarify which tasks could be delegated to which person or department. This was actually a rather distributed model that had the president and board of directors at the centre, with those who had the information (those closest to the operation) being given the most responsibility.

In the early twentieth century, the model started to look more like a traditional hierarchy, illustrated by The Tabulating Machine Company's Organisational Chart of 1917.[33] (The Tabulating Machine Company is now known as IBM.) Conventional organisational structures push decision-making and power up the hierarchy. The more senior you are, the more power you have. Seniority usually means you are trusted with bigger budgets, look after more people and have access to more information. Even so, everyone is answerable to someone, even the CEO. There is always someone who can block you from doing what you want to do, who needs to be persuaded (because you need their permission) and who holds your future in their hands.

Hierarchical structures are meant to organise people and activities so that everyone knows what they are doing as part of a predictable process. When all the moving parts operate successfully, it's like a well-oiled machine. If people respect that they are cogs and wheels within a machine, everything will run smoothly, people won't become problematic and there will be consistency... as if a machine was doing the work.

Of course, people are not machines. They do not show up to work and operate within a clearly defined remit. They have feelings about what they are being asked to do. They see problems with it. They have ideas of their own. Maybe they don't like their manager, their teammates or colleagues from somewhere else in the business, and this creates friction in the system. They want to be recognised for their contribution. They want the chance to advance in their careers. Some days they won't really be feeling it. Sometimes they will want to try something new and operate outside the confines of the role they've been ascribed.

Equally, these days we also expect people to operate outside of their strict remit. The system was built for compliance, but today we want people to do what we say while also sharing their ideas, thinking outside the box, collaborating, problem-solving and taking risks. We need them to do more than rock up, operate like a robot and then go home. We need their brain, their whole self, because the challenges facing us are more complex and the solutions required are more sophisticated than they were in the Industrial Age.

Organising people like they are machines doing repetitive actions all day works pretty well when people are doing repetitive actions all day. When we want and need human ingenuity and heart for our organisations to succeed, however, then it doesn't make sense to organise them like they are parts in a machine.

Remember those two Victorian-Age beliefs? They are baked into the hierarchy in many ways:

- People are second-rate machines, so we organise them as such.

- People can't be trusted so they need to be given permission by someone more trustworthy further up the line.

- People can't be trusted to handle complex and potentially scary information so we keep that information from them, for their own good, and to give those higher up more power.

- People are second-rate machines who should ideally leave their emotions at the door when they come to work and do as they are told.

- People are second-rate machines and their work should be predictable, measurable and controllable like a machine's. The hierarchy is the most predictable, measurable and controllable structure.

- People can't be trusted so we empower managers to hold them to account, provide feedback, assign tasks and supervise their activity. Those managers are themselves managed by someone with more authority to keep an eye on them and keep them in line.

- People lower down the hierarchy are less trusted than those higher up, so those higher up are given decision-making authority. Those lower down must report information from the ground to those at the top so that those at the top can decide what to do about problems or opportunities.

- People cannot be trusted, so even if tasks or responsibilities are delegated to them, the manager retains the right to step in and correct bad decisions.

Let me reassure you. I know you are an enlightened leader who understands that people are not machines, and I know that you recognise that, in today's world and the uncertain future we face, the old Victorian mentality will inhibit our organisations from doing what they are here to do and will turn off our best people – the people who contribute the most to making the organisation thrive.

No matter how enlightened you are, though, in a hierarchical system with hierarchical hardwiring baked for 250 years into how we work, the gravitational pull is always towards a chain of command, a command and control style of management, and humans being considered second-rate, untrustworthy machines.

Before I tell you what to do about this, I want to show you why hierarchical thinking is such a significant barrier to liberating the talent of our people.

Hierarchy and accountability

I recall sitting with a coaching client (let's call her Susan) who was confused as to why her team weren't as concerned about the quality of their work as she was. She had hired talented designers and writers for her marketing department but their work often contained mistakes or was incomplete. She wanted to know how to get them to take quality as seriously as she did, particularly when the work was going to be presented to the board or to a client.

She also struggled with her hours, noting that she often only got to her own work in the evenings or at weekends because her days were spent fixing up other people's work so that it met the required standards.

Susan signed off everyone's work, and because the quality was poor, she felt even more responsibility to check it. After all, what if a client saw a mistake? As the leader of the team, she felt it was her job to ensure that whatever was produced by her team was perfect. What she couldn't understand was why they didn't care about it as much as she did.

In a hierarchical system, managers hold on to final decision-making power. They say they have delegated and that they want to empower, but that empowerment is conditional: 'Show me that you can do the work to the standard expected and, if you prove you can, I will let you do more.' They check their team's work to ensure it is good enough. They feel this is how they add value. It's what they are there for.

As a consequence, the people in their team know that any mistakes will be caught.

Susan always seemed to find something wrong with her team's work – whether it was a missing full stop, the order of the slides or some of the wording. When the team saw the final presentation, Susan had not only corrected mistakes but tweaked it in various ways. If, Susan reasoned, she was going through the presentation deck anyway, she might as well move a few pieces around to make it more to her liking. Furthermore, knowing her own boss would be aware that she'd been through it, she had to show she was doing her job and prove she knew what a good presentation looked like. She had to put her stamp on it.

The result? The team never felt the pain of a mistake because Susan always caught it. They were never held to account. They never had to stand in front of the client with a typo they had missed on the slide behind their head. Why would they check and re-check when Susan was going to do it anyway? And, as Susan never seemed satisfied with what they'd done, they lost faith in their ability to get it 'right'. They tried doing it her way, but she still wasn't satisfied. They gave up.

This is how learnt dependency is created. The team didn't trust themselves. They didn't understand how to do what Susan wanted. They weren't going to waste any more time on it knowing she'd got their backs. The cycle continued.

This is how our modern hierarchy works.

The structure is mechanical. Just look at a modern org chart – people fitting into boxes, straight lines connecting roles with other roles like an assembly line. But we've already established that people are not machines and roles are ever-changing.

Most companies get hung up on the organisational structure, believing that there is a right structure if only they can find it, but there isn't a right structure. As long as you have hierarchical hardwiring, you're going to be inefficient, you're going to create repetition and busy-work, you're going to disempower, you're going to be slow, you're going to make poor decisions that don't work on the ground, you're going to have politics, exclusion and favouritism, and you're going to prevent people from doing the work that makes the difference.

The authors of a fantastic *Harvard Business Review* article[34] describe how most of us are doing two jobs – the one we've been paid for and the second unpaid job of managing our reputations and hiding our inadequacies from others and ourselves. The hierarchy reinforces this double life.

People spend a great deal of their time making sure they are seen in a positive light. They want to be thought of as hard-working, committed, ambitious, proud of the organisation, on board with its vision, in alignment with its values, admiring of the senior leadership team, willing to take risks (but not make mistakes), and expert in their field.

At the same time, human nature is that they don't want to be controlled. They want autonomy. They don't want to be constantly answerable to a higher authority. They want to be treated like adults, trusted to do a good job and allowed to get on with it.

But what about when something goes wrong?

Well, that's when problems arise.

Because, in a hierarchy, no one is ever actually accountable. If I mess up, my manager will take the heat on my behalf. My manager can get their manager to take the heat or blame another team. Accountability can often be pushed up to the top where, inevitably, it is pushed back down, or sideways to another team who then pushes it somewhere else like a never-ending game of pass the parcel. Perhaps the music stops at some point, and someone is fired or reprimanded, but the system persists – because it's convenient.

(I'm going to use the terms *responsible* and *accountable* here. They have very specific meanings. Responsibility is about the task. I am responsible for putting the laundry on at home. It's my job. Accountability is about what happens with the result – who takes ownership of the outcome? If I accidentally shrink the clothes, am I accountable? It depends. Was there a label that said I couldn't tumble dry the item? Did I read it? Was it clearly written? It was my teenaged daughter's jumper. If I make a mistake with her sweater, is she the one accountable? No one really knows! Hence, no one is accountable and the blame for the shrunken jumper can be batted back and forth endlessly.)

In a hierarchy, tasks are assigned and, when this is done clearly, people know what they are responsible for, but who is accountable? That's more difficult to establish because hierarchies are about teamwork, collaboration and co-ownership. We are all in this together. There's no 'I' in team. *We* decide.

Let's look at some situations:

- A discussion takes place in a team about the best way forward. There are different opinions. The most senior person listens and decides based on what they've heard. Is that person accountable if the decision turns out to be flawed?

- An individual contributor has an idea. They go to their manager and seek approval to implement it. The manager says, 'Yes, but if you run into problems, come and see me and we can work out what to do.' Who is accountable?

- A team can't make a unanimous agreement about the way forward and decide that the majority wins. The people in the team who didn't agree were asked to adopt cabinet responsibility. What if that decision turns out to be a bad one? Who is accountable?

- Your manager delegates a project to you with clear deliverables and timeframes and you agree to take it on. Who is accountable?

Hierarchy and conventional hierarchical structures mean it is hard to pinpoint an individual who is accountable for anything. Therefore no one is account-able. It's a matter of debate, always.

I'm not saying people don't care. I know you'll have had sleepless nights worrying about work, about something that's not going to plan, or about how you're going to make a great idea a reality. It's not a personal lack of commitment.

It's just that hierarchy gets in the way of adult-adult conversations and consequences.

It's too easy to hide. You know your manager is going to advocate for you. She doesn't want you to look bad because it makes her look bad. That means loyalty to your manager and to your team becomes more important than speaking your truth. You might not want to give your manager tough feedback because you want her to have your back if you get something wrong. You may not agree with a decision made by the team, but you don't want to speak up because, in other circumstances, you might need the team to support you in public.

This also reinforces siloes because teams are trying to present themselves in a good light. If a team can make it look like another team was to blame then they've diverted attention away from their own shortcomings. Some teams are easy to blame. They are a bit chaotic, maybe their leader isn't good at advocating for the team or doesn't have the ear of a more senior leader.

You want ownership and to be treated like an adult but, still, it's always handy to have your manager there to take the heat, just in case. Accountability is diluted.

Even if you are the kind of person who is willing to put up your hand, like an adult, and say, 'I was accountable for that and I should be the one under scrutiny here', it's not that clear cut. You've been the bigger person, but we all know it wasn't just you. There was a series of decisions and behaviours that led to the outcome and it would be unfair to blame you. This is especially true if you are of great value to the business. No one wants you to pay the price for a mistake when it leaves the business without one of its valued leaders.

This system doesn't work well for the business. By doing this second job of protecting your team or protecting yourself, you don't always make the best decisions. You don't speak uncomfortable truths. You don't call out behaviour, particularly the behaviour of senior people, because of the risk to you. You don't want to be locked out of the room where decisions are made. You don't want information to be withheld from you, and you may not want the burden of being ultimately accountable, even if you say you do.

Parent–teenager dynamics

The hierarchy creates parents and children. We are always asking for permission or granting permission. We are always playing Mum off against Dad. We are honing our negotiating skills, keeping our cards close to our chests, looking for weakness or power.

If we are honest, we want a lot of freedom at work but we also want protection, so it's not a parent-child dynamic but a parent-teenager dynamic.

Just as with my laundry situation above, my teen daughter wants the freedom to make her own decisions but also expects her laundry to be done and her dinner made for her. That's what I see in most organisations. People say they want autonomy but they also want someone else to refer up to, to hide behind, and to be accountable if something goes wrong.

The role of manager is often mistaken for the role of parent, to protect the reputation of their people and stand up for them when something goes wrong. The manager might even say, 'Hands up, I will take the bullet on this one', but because everyone knows they are protecting someone in their team and that they didn't make a mistake, they get a stern talking to and are told to get more control over the actions of their team members. Ultimately, though, there are no consequences.

Shades of grey

Shades of grey are often dangerous in an organisation. When there is a vacuum of information, a lack of clarity about roles or responsibilities or accountabilities, in floods speculation, usually of the worst kind. Things fall through the cracks. You get duplication. You get people feeling threatened, people playing games, seeking proximity to power, a way to protect their reputation, to hide from consequences.

When you have shades of grey, decisions don't turn into actions. You think you've made decisions and assigned ownership, but nothing happens, or it happens but not in the way agreed.

The value of the human workforce today comes from our ability to debate the rights and wrongs of a situation, from speaking our minds to enrich a discussion, or understanding how another person's perspective differs from our own in order to create an inclusive solution. We cannot play by the Industrial-Age rules of the hierarchy. We need to move at pace because, if we don't, the solution that was right for conditions six months ago is no longer suited for the conditions today. We can't have time lags. We can't allow the noise of busy-work, pleasing the boss, staying safe and wasting time reporting up and down, to get in the way of serving our customers and clients in innovative ways. Hierarchy is simply too slow.

The power gradient

David Marquet describes the power gradient as the social distance between one person and another.[35] Hierarchy makes it harder for a junior person to tell someone senior something they don't want to hear than it is for a more senior person to tell someone junior. While you may believe you have an open-door policy and have encouraged more junior people to tell you what's on their minds, they will be reluctant to do so because of the power gradient. You, after all, are their protector. You can have their back… or not. You will be the one signing off on their proposals. You will be deciding their bonus and their promotion readiness. You will be the one to decide how much autonomy to give them.

If they displease you by saying something that is hard for you to hear, their world becomes a little less safe.

You, on the other hand, have less at stake by speaking your truth to them. So what if they feel uncomfortable, exposed or embarrassed? Even if you are trying to protect their feelings, it is partly your job to provide feedback and critique. You may give this feedback sensitively but, if they react badly, that's their problem, not yours.

Don't forget, you're fighting 250 years of hierarchical hardwiring here. It isn't your fault. At school, the job is to please the teacher, to hand in your work on time, to sit quietly, to raise your hand to ask a question, to get the 'right' answer. Even opinions are learnt by studying the opinions of others and then repeating those opinions, crediting your sources.

Growing up we are encouraged to conform and fit in. I remember wearing a particularly uncomfortable suit during an internship at a legal firm in my teens. My dad picked it out. I was meant to dress like a lawyer although I was sixteen years old, it was the mid-eighties and my preference was backcombed hair and a floor-length Goth skirt. We are taught how to describe our strengths and weaknesses in interviews (making our weaknesses palatable to the interview board). We are told to be enthusiastic. At school, we are given an effort grade as well as an attainment grade and expected to show equal enthusiasm for a maths class as a cookery class. No matter how you feel about a subject, look keen.

No surprise that young people arrive in the workplace ready to be compliant and diligent students who do what they are told. Now we are seeing a new generation, Gen Z, joining the workplace. They may be less impressed with your job title and your years of experience. They may feel they have the right to speak up and speak out, particularly when they observe injustice or intolerance.

However, this is very much at odds with the conventional workplace culture. After a few years in a typical company environment, they may learn, like a lot of other people, that their opinions fall on deaf ears and get in the way of their desire to make a difference.

Even if they are willing to keep trying, unless you embrace a different approach, we will be waiting for two or three more generations for change to happen. If we want and need cultures where people can enhance the richness of a debate, where it is important that people speak up, in the moment, so that the organisation can adapt in real time to new information, and where the value of people is their humanity rather than their compliance, we can't wait until today's Gen Zs are in charge in twenty years.

You will have to do something different now.

Proximity to power

In a system based on hierarchy, power is unevenly distributed. Those at the top officially have more, so cosying up to the most powerful makes sense. If your manager doesn't have enough power, their boss might. If your boss holds your future in their hands you want to ensure you have their attention. One of the challenges of hybrid working is that it's harder to achieve physical proximity to power. If you aren't there every day but someone else is, they get seen by the powerful people in the staff kitchen, arriving early at the meeting while you're still trying to join virtually, going for a drink after work or simply sitting diligently at their desk.

This power differential leads to politics, as different power-players face off against each other, seeing who can win battles for territory (a larger team, more resources, more credit). Because influencing senior people becomes such an important part of the culture (because you need their permission to do anything), people become highly skilled at manipulation, reputation-building, persuasion and sales. It's not the best idea that gets signed off, but the one that was presented best. Certain personalities thrive in this environment, while others struggle regardless of the calibre of their contribution.

Information is power. People withhold information to ensure they have an advantage over other colleagues. In this way, information is locked in disparate parts of the organisation, with HR having access to some data while the finance team has other data, for instance. Each party believes they can make a compelling case and prove their value by presenting information that the other party doesn't have. Rather than collaborating, teams compete.

When I was a BBC journalist, we had a big whiteboard on which we would keep our emerging running order for the next day's programme, with the guests and stories we would be covering and their timeslots, but the whiteboard was only partially true. Other news programmes on the same network could see our board and we didn't want them to scoop us, so we would occasionally lie or miss certain guests from the board so that our 'colleagues' on *The World at One* or *PM* wouldn't steal them from under us. We all worked for the BBC, and we were all in the business of informing, educating and entertaining, but we also wanted to break stories and get the credit for breaking stories. That meant ensuring colleagues on other shows didn't get there first. So now you know.

A waste of time and energy

Circumnavigating the system, playing politics, trying to keep people engaged in a dysfunctional system, influencing, reporting up and down, waiting for decisions to be made which you will then have to implement, discovering that work has slipped through the cracks or that two teams have been trying to implement a similar idea before each other to get the credit... all of this takes time and energy. As explained in the article mentioned earlier, 'Making Business Personal', it's a second job that is as time-consuming, if not more so, than the job we've been paid to do.[36]

Just imagine if we took away even half of this activity. How many meetings could be cancelled? How much more efficiently could decisions be made and enacted? How much conflict could be avoided? How much richer would discussions be?

What would happen if the focus was entirely on getting the best outcome for the customer or client because there was no need to duck and dive internally?

When you hand in that laptop on the last day of your working career, do you want to leave behind a system that requires people to do this second job, which is a massive distraction from the true mission and purpose of the organisation? Do you maintain the status quo because it's worked well for you? Or would you be willing to give something away – power, status, being admired – in order to change things, and are you willing to pay that price? Would you prefer to hold on to your power, collude with the system because you've done well as a result, and hand over a system that's been outdated for decades to the next generation?

Action 3: Give away decision-making authority

As long as you hold on to final decision-making authority, you will be reinforcing the hierarchy and the dysfunctional behaviours which thrive as a result. We hold on to decision-making in subtle ways:

- When people come to us to sign off on their idea, we make tweaks or suggestions, often because we feel that's how we add value, but what we've reinforced is their incapacity to make decisions without us and our authority to 'improve' their work.

- We make people prove their decisions to us, asking them to talk through their thinking or sell the options to us with a recommendation. We do not insist they sit with the discomfort of making the final decision.

- We trust some people with decisions but not others, making it unclear what the expectation is and undermining the confidence of those we don't trust and who can see clearly that they are treated differently from their more-trusted colleagues.

- We have meetings at which people update us, passing information up to us so we can advocate on their behalf or simply pass on a summarised version to our own bosses, who will use that summary to make a decision which is then passed down.

- We hold on to certain decisions without asking if there is another way. We decide on promotion prospects for people in our team whether or not we know much about what they do or how well they do it. We hold on to financial decisions. We continue to sign off expenses. We attempt to solve the big issues on our own. We see someone struggling and we try to fix it for them. We see people are busy and stressed so we roll up our sleeves and take on more ourselves (whether they've asked us to or not).

- When people are struggling with a decision, even if we've told them it is theirs to make, we rescue them and decide for them. We don't want them to suffer.

All of this reinforces the idea that, somehow, we are better than them. We are superhuman. We are the parent. We are all-knowing and infallible. We are right.

To break the hierarchy, you have to let go of being right, being 'better than'. You have to recognise that you have information and experience but your job isn't to gather information from others, combine it with your information and experience and then make a decision. It is to give away all the information and experience you have, add it to the pot and let them make the final call.

You are a tool they can access.

Your job is to assist them in their thinking but hold lightly to your way of doing things. It is, after all, only one way of many. You may think you're helping by reducing the pain and discomfort they would feel if the decision was theirs and theirs alone, but in fact you are delaying their learning. You are getting in the way of their growth. Whatever the outcome of the decision, this is the best time to learn from it. Otherwise, they will need to learn it later.

I repeat, you aren't superhuman. If you can take the strain of making a decision, so can they.

Now, this doesn't mean dumping decisions on people and abdicating responsibility. You have to ensure they are the right person to decide. Do they have the experience to make a good decision here? Are they ready for this responsibility? Do they know how decisions like this are made, and what factors need to be taken into account? Is this their job or someone else's?

Someone with six months of experience in their career is going to be making different kinds of decisions than someone with six years of experience, but that doesn't mean they can't decide anything. What level of decision-making sits with this role and this level of experience? More importantly, what's your role in enhancing their ability to take on more decision-making responsibilities? If you make decisions for them for the next three years, will they be in a better position to take over more decision-making by then, or will they be just as dependent on you as they are now? Will they, in that time, have learnt that they might as well just do what you say? Will they have stopped thinking? Will they have stopped coming to you with ideas? Will they have developed some work-around and be gaming the system so they can have some influence over their work? Will they keep you out of the loop? Will they come to you for everything?

In the next three years, what bad habits will you have taught them simply because you were trying to protect them from the discomfort of learning for themselves?

Whenever you can, push decision-making down as low as you dare – and then dare to push it lower. Provide people with the information they need and then let them decide. If it turns out that the decision didn't work as planned, support them in thinking afresh and having another go.

At first, they won't trust that you mean it. They've been taught that you get paid the big bucks because you're the one who decides. They think that you'll step in and rescue them if they head down the wrong path. They think you'll catch those typos and that lazy thinking before it goes to the board, but if you consistently refuse to collude with these beliefs they will, in time, come to believe that you mean it.

When they come to you asking you to cast your eye over their proposal, refuse. Instead, ask questions like:

- What other information do you need to feel confident enough to go ahead?
- What are you hoping I will say?

- What are the risks and can you live with them?

- How could you mitigate the risks?

- Who else do you need input from before you decide?

- When would it be helpful for us to check in again?

With all these questions, you are leaving accountability firmly with them. You aren't expecting them to convince you, or even explain their thinking unless they would find it useful to verbalise it before deciding. Sometimes people need to hear their thoughts aloud.

As you notice a tension in the pit of your stomach and a voice in your head saying, 'I wouldn't do it this way... I wish I could just tweak this little thing... I'm not adding any value unless I improve this idea with my own', you remind yourself that you aren't right, just different. Your job isn't to coax them to your way of thinking but to give them to tools to think for themselves.

In time, they will learn that your job isn't that of a parent, or teacher, or all-knowing superhuman or protector. You are a thinking partner, wise counsel at best, another adult with whom they can explore their ideas and access information they need, before deciding something for themselves. Then they will learn that they live with the consequences of the decisions they've made. That's how they learn and grow. That's how they get a true sense that they make a difference. That's also how you break the hierarchy which keeps people operating like second-rate machines so that they can become the first-rate humans they are capable of becoming.

Final word: Breaking systemic hierarchies

This chapter has focused on what you, as one individual, can do differently. Ultimately, if you want to leave the world better than you found it, you may need to be more radical. In my interview with Chris May, you will hear how he and his colleagues at their organisation, Mayden, have created a company without managers. He will describe how he catches himself leaning on his authority as the founder of the business, and how the people in the organisation must still consciously resist their tendency to create a hierarchy, even in this manager-free system.

They persist because they believe hierarchy gets in the way of service to the customer. They are driven by the desire to do the best job they can for the people they serve and by a belief that people contribute the most when they are treated like people, not like machines.

Mayden has continually revised and refined how it organises people and projects. It hasn't found the perfect system and nor does it attempt to. People in the business are just paying attention and addressing tensions as they find them.

It's not my job here to convince you to adopt self-management, but I encourage you to read up and have conversations and get curious about the opportunity that self-management or, at least, less management, presents.

Start talking about it with colleagues, start experimenting and see what comes up for you. Our ego is challenged when we consider breaking the hierarchy, particularly when we consider dismantling it entirely. After all, if you are in a position of authority in your organisation, you've been a beneficiary of the hierarchical system. Now I'm suggesting that you give away the power you've accumulated. More than that, I'm asking you to consider dismantling that whole system, starting with your own team and then engaging with other leaders to change the hardwiring from hierarchical to communal. In my interview with Diederick Janse, we discuss organisations as communities and employees as citizens, so check that out as well.

This 'letting go' of authority is a personal development journey, not a structural change, but it's one of the biggest areas of growth for most of today's leaders. It needs to be a priority if you are to change the culture of work and re-contract with the people employed by your organisation in a way that makes sense in this fast-changing business context.

LISTEN NOW

Chris May is the founder of Mayden, a tech business which supports healthcare services. Mayden is a 'self-managing organisation', although it didn't start that way. In our conversation, Chris talks about some of the challenges he has faced as he continues to work on his willingness to distribute decision-making and step away from the conventional role of founder and CEO.

You can listen to the interview at **www. buzzsprout.com/2250059/13664547** or listen to any of the other interviews here: **https:// punksinsuitshowtoleadtheworkplacereformation. buzzsprout.com**

Summary

Hierarchy reinforces the belief that people are second-rate machines and cannot be trusted. We can remove layers of hierarchy, but the behaviours will persist unless we change the dynamic and give away decision-making authority. If we want people to think for themselves (and we need them to think for themselves to get the true value from them), we have to break the traditional behaviours that get in the way of thinking. The hierarchy was created to prevent people from thinking for themselves, after all!

Your job isn't to be superhuman or have all the answers, even if people want you to perform this role. Instead, you are going to push decision-making as low as you dare and then support people in learning how to make good decisions for themselves.

Questions to consider

- What decisions do I hold on to?

- What could I give away?

- When do I step in to 'rescue people' and what would happen if I stopped?

- Do I act like I am better or wiser than others? Is that true?

- What information do I hold on to which I could share? What stops me?

- What would my role be if it wasn't the decision-maker?

- How else do I reinforce hierarchy because it makes me feel good?

- How else do I reinforce hierarchy to protect people from discomfort?

- How else do I game the system myself for my benefit?

- What could I do differently to break this archaic system?

- Who else could I engage with to break the hierarchy at a more systemic level?

CHAPTER 4

LEADERSHIP

Leadership
Not Born To Run

This chapter isn't a definitive guide to every theory on leadership (with my analysis about what's wrong with them all) or a list of all the qualities a leader needs to justify the title 'leader'. There are enough *Harvard Business Review* articles detailing the myriad qualities leaders 'need', and literally thousands of books trying to distil what makes someone a leader down to a list of 'dos' and 'don'ts'.

Instead, this chapter is a plea, directed at you, to think about what is required of you to lead the change I'm describing in this book. There is a specific role you need to play if you want to leave the world of work – and the world in general – a better place because of the kind of leader you were at this stage in your career. I'm going to describe it here and I beg you to consider embodying it.

There is also a question you'll need to reflect on. Because you may already be a 'leader' in your organisation. What I describe here might be so different, and so unappealing compared with what you do now, that you might put the book down at this stage and seek inspiration elsewhere.

At the end of this chapter, you'll have to ask yourself: 'Do I really want to do this?'

Do I accept the challenge? Am I willing to change, perhaps dramatically, and let go of my current concept of what a leader does and what a leader is? Or would I rather keep doing what I've been doing and reaping the rewards… the ego boost, the respect and status, the feeling of power and superiority and, perhaps, the reward of getting things done and seeing my fingerprints all over everything?

We have created a largely dysfunctional (or at least, mis-functional) way of working which inhibits people from doing their best work. It burns people out, turns people off, requires huge sacrifice and doesn't always get the best outcome for clients, customers or the wider community. This is happening at a time when change is so fast and so momentous that, unless we fundamentally reconsider how we use the talent of human beings, our businesses will be unable to operate.

If you believe this too, that means you'll have to do something different. You'll have to lead differently.

What kind of leadership do we need from you right now?

The kind of leaders we need now are those who create an environment where people can do their best work in pursuit of the mission or purpose of the organisation.

We currently have a situation where people struggle to do their best work. The culture, the systems, the management structure, the technology, the ways decisions are made, the ways budgets are allocated, the ways goals are set, the ways people are seen and treated and much more besides – all of this contributes to a suboptimal environment, a dangerous environment for people's health and well-being, as well as an environment that cannot get the best outcomes for customers and clients and other stakeholders.

When people achieve something great, as they frequently do, it is despite the environment not because of it. That's not your fault – you are as much a product of this system as anyone, but if leadership today is about one thing, it is about dismantling that suboptimal system.

If you avoid making the necessary changes, all you are doing is plastering over the cracks in a fundamentally broken system. Of course, you can't dismantle this whole system at once. It's going to require tweaks, adaptations, projects and programmes, but the leadership required of you now is based on a dogged commitment to creating an environment where people can do their best work in pursuit of the mission or purpose of the organisation.

Let's break that down.

A word about mission and purpose

If your organisation's mission or purpose is unclear, or there is a public version (a mission that sounds admirable) and a true version (a less admirable mission which is never overtly stated but which drives most behaviour and decisions), this might be where you have to start. If you don't have the authority in the organisation as a whole, you may have to set your sights lower and start with the mission or purpose of your small corner of the organisation instead, but whether you like the mission or purpose of the organisation or not, all organisations have them. All organisations exist for a reason, even if that reason is to make the owners richer. That's a valid purpose. It's just that companies aren't always honest about their true purpose, which can lead to confusing decisions and agendas.

In Chapter 6, I will return to this topic. For now, let's assume that your organisation has a mission or purpose that is at the least benign if not inspiring, and that you are happy to get behind that mission in your role as a leader.

Caretakers of the mission, purpose and ethos of the organisation

Old-style leaders were assumed to be visionaries. They were the ones with the Big Idea, who could imagine, describe and sell a future state which inspired others to follow. That's a whole bundle of talents which are pretty superhuman.

This idea leads many people to feel they cannot be 'leaders' because they don't think that way (they can't always picture a fully-formed future reality), or they don't know what the right vision is (they don't know enough to generate the 'right' idea), or they aren't influential communicators (they are more reserved, they don't have the words, or they don't enjoy addressing groups).

The truth is that sometimes you'll be able to picture what the future could look like and sometimes you won't. Sometimes you may be at the table when the purpose or mission is generated, and sometimes you won't. Sometimes the picture of the future will come from others, from people with expertise in different areas to you or from different contributors adding different elements. Sometimes that purpose or mission will have been in the organisation before you arrived.

To 'lead' doesn't necessarily imply that you generated the Big Ideas or the vision of the future.

What differentiates a leader today from an old-style leader is a willingness to hold up that mission, purpose and ethos at times when it could easily be forgotten or when it is uncomfortable to remember it. Picture yourself standing on the horizon, waving a beacon and reminding people, 'This is what we are heading towards!' If you aren't there, doing that, people will look at what is directly in front of them. They may forget the bigger context for making good decisions. They may make decisions that are of short-term benefit but that divert the organisation from its longer-term path. They may make decisions with benefits today but with costs stored up for later. Working towards a mission or purpose while staying aligned with the ethos of the organisation is often a difficult and painful journey. Without you holding that beacon up, it's too easy for people to get lost when the going gets tough.

By mission or purpose, I really mean 'service'. Who is the organisation here to serve? Customers? Clients? The wider community? What is it here to do? For whom? Yes, a commercial organisation is meant to make money, otherwise it ceases to exist, but beyond that, what is it for?

Not everyone will join an organisation because they care deeply about its mission. It may not be their life purpose. Everyone works for different reasons and with different motivations. Demanding that everyone cares deeply about the organisation's mission inevitably leads to dishonesty, but that's not why you have a mission. You have a mission because, without one, there is no shared focus of attention. There is no collective outcome, no shared sense of what success looks like. Nonhuman employees don't need a collective focus. They deal in facts and data. But for humans to work together, to be more than the sum of their parts, they need to know what the organisation exists to do, who it exists to serve and see a clear organisational purpose. They need to be able to say, 'Sure, I can get behind that.' This is the unifying beacon that determines what they are working towards together.

By ethos, I mean what the organisation stands for, its values, and the way it goes about delivering that 'service'. Every organisation has its own 'feel'. Some are clearly at one end of a spectrum or the other – for instance, highly empowering or highly controlling. The vast majority are somewhere in the middle. You may note that most organisations you've worked for have ended up feeling roughly the same. That is because we've become stuck with quite a narrow sense of 'normal' based on a Victorian model, as described previously in this book.

I expect that organisational ethos will become more and more important as leaders like you start to release us from those Victorian shackles. At the very least, if people can work from home and for an organisation based anywhere in the world, what makes working for one organisation feel different to working for another? If they are interchangeable, where is the loyalty or the commitment to the mission? In the past, perhaps the office environment was a differentiator. Maybe the company served a decent lunch or was located close to bars or restaurants, or close to your home. When we take that out of the equation, something else has to differentiate you in order to attract great people to come and be part of the mission.

For people to do their best work, they need to feel safe. A guiding ethos provides people with consistency, and this is an important part of that sense of safety – knowing how things work, the criteria that are used to make decisions, how they can expect to be treated and how they are expected to treat others.

Inconsistency leads to a lack of safety and lack of safety does not enable people to do their best work.

Beyond that, ethos is becoming a differentiator for customers and clients too. Brand trust is a key determiner of buying decisions[37] with more and more people saying they want the organisations they buy from to share their values.[38] That doesn't just mean the values you put on your website or the values you proclaim in your advertising, but how you treat people, how you run your organisation, your ethics and your ESG credentials. All of this tracks back to your ethos and your willingness to stand for what you stand for, even when it is hard to do and even when there is a price to pay for being true to that ethos.

The mission or purpose and the ethos of the organisation should create a tension. There is 'what is' and 'what could be'. There is the current state and the future state. By holding that future state 'beacon', you will create discomfort because you will highlight the gap between what is and what could be, what is and what the organisation is setting out to be and do.

As is the case with horizons, as the organisation moves forward, the horizon continues to move back, so there is always a tension.

In this way, a leader isn't just a facilitator. They aren't neutral. They have an agenda. They hold a position – standing on the horizon, waving that beacon about so no one forgets where we're going.

This can be uncomfortable. It's easy to set out a Big Idea, a mission or a purpose and articulate the organisation's ethos in theoretical terms, but living that ethos, moving constantly towards it, facing up to the barriers that inevitably arise and addressing them head-on is uncomfortable. By holding the beacon, you will be the focus of that discomfort. People won't like it, but if you ignore the brave, enlightened intention behind the mission, purpose and ethos to avoid the discomfort, then you aren't really leading, are you?

More about tension

As I've just said, holding the beacon creates a tension between what is and what could be.

Within that big tension are smaller tensions. In order to create an environment where people can come and do their best work, you'll have to seek out these tensions. Where is the 'friction', where the way you do things now isn't optimal? Unfortunately, that's going to be pretty much everything:

- How you hold meetings, what meetings you have, who is in those meetings

- Working hours, employment contracts, bonuses, salaries and rewards

- Office design, flexible and hybrid working approaches

- Organisational structure and hierarchy

- Decision-making

- Technology and how it is used

127

- Communication including formal internal comms, listening, engagement, empowerment
- Culture, acceptable or tolerated behaviours, diversity of opinions, perspectives and working styles
- Growth and development, advancement, attraction and retention, onboarding, use of talent
- Creativity and idea generation
- Client relationships and contracting
- Business development and business growth, targets and goals, budgets

I could go on. In every corner of your organisation there will be stuff that doesn't work well. What stops people from doing their best work? What stops you?

We tend to work around tensions. Sometimes those workarounds are so embedded in the organisation that we don't even think of them as workarounds. A process may be complex and time-consuming, but it's become so normal that we don't question whether it can be done another way, or whether that system or process exists simply because we don't trust people and we just want them to behave like machines. Sometimes a complex process exists because technology isn't really up to the task or because we are trying to circumnavigate a specific person or department. Sometimes a complex process exists because it works in our favour, giving us and our team more power or resources.

But what if our attention was tuned into enabling people to come and do their best work in service of the bigger mission or purpose of the organisation? We need leaders to go towards tensions, to spot them or to pay attention when other people spot them. Go towards discomfort rather than finding a workaround.

Much of the politics, busy-work, complexity and inefficiency in an organisation comes from work-arounds. When we step over a tension, we simply kick it down the road where it gathers momentum and volume. The next time we meet it, it is hairier and uglier than the last time and requires even more effort to work around. Eventually, you have no choice but to face it… only now it's huge and has cost the organisation time, energy, broken relationships and financial pain for years. Stepping over tensions and leaving them for future-you (or whatever mug is in your role by then) isn't leadership. Better to do something about it now.

'Best work': What does that mean?

Everyone has talents. They may be talents that are highly regarded in our society – running fast, playing the piano well, turning a pile of wood into a beautiful armoire – skills that people have a natural affinity for and have developed further. They may be talents related more to personal qualities – being kind, being a great friend, having a way with words. They may be attitudes – dedicated, hard-working, detail-oriented. They may be values – commitment to family, desire for lifelong learning, community, giving back. They may also be unknown to the person because they've never had a chance to identify or develop them, or because their particular talent has never been valued.

There are many qualities in humans that we undervalue or that we try to suffocate because they don't fit with a rather narrow perspective on what has value and what doesn't. Until recently, any show of emotion at work was considered unprofessional. We are now starting to understand that shows of emotion at work have value (see Chapter 5 for more on this). We talk about emotional intelligence, resilience, authenticity and speaking from the heart in a way that previous generations would have been uncomfortable with. This means talents based on self-awareness, being empathetic and being a good listener are valued in a way that they weren't in previous generations.

But the way we view 'talent' is still rather limited. For this reason, many people feel they are nothing special, that they have nothing of value to offer.

However, as we move towards organisations where nonhuman and human employees work side by side, we need to think differently about talent. If people can't come and do their best work, bringing every talent they have to that endeavour, then we aren't getting maximum value from them. If people can't develop their talents or if they keep their talents hidden, it is possible that a bot could do their job. It is the very complexity that humans bring to work that differentiates them from the bots.

Today's leaders must create an environment where people can do their best work, and that includes helping them develop *all* their talents. Growth and development are critical parts of that. If a person can't grow, their talent is stunted, and if they can't bring their talent to their work, you can't do your job. You don't have all the answers in every situation. You need people in the organisation who can draw on their talent to solve problems that you can't, in pursuit of the mission or purpose of the organisation.

Does your style of leadership today liberate the talent of people around you or limit it? Are you dedicated to helping them become the best they can be, or are you a barrier to that? Does your ego insist that you have to be 'the best', or can it embrace others being better than you?

Do you create space for people's talents to be taken to their maximum? This includes your own talents.

And do you wonder, as I describe this type of leadership, whether this is where your talents lie?

We need to untangle leadership from seniority, experience and technical expertise. The kind of leaders we need today may not have the seniority, or the experience or the technical expertise of 'leaders' in days gone by. Just because you are senior doesn't automatically make you talented in the areas I'm describing here.

The kind of leaders we need may not have exceptional technical expertise. Certainly, they may not be as talented as the people around them in this way, but what they have is a particular talent for creating an environment where people can come and do their best work in pursuit of the mission or purpose of the organisation.

Leadership has become a status symbol, but the kind of leadership I'm describing isn't necessarily high status. There isn't necessarily a lot of glory in it. In creating space for others to do their best work, you might not get the credit. It is others who will shine, but the difference that this kind of leader makes is greater than any one individual contributor can make because this kind of leader looks for the barriers that are stopping people doing their best work and liberates their talent. That's where its meaning comes from, and that requires a set of talents which have been vastly undervalued in the working world. Until now.

'Best work' also means the best ideas and best decisions

Part of liberating people's talent so they can do their best work is enabling the best thinking.

Until now, we've associated leadership with being the creator of the vision, that somehow the leader is the originator of the vision. That assumes that the leader always knows the best thing to do, the best decision, the best direction to go. That might not be the case. Instead, they might be the enablers of *other* people's ideas, their role being to create a space where others can create and innovate.

What are the barriers to 'best ideas' and 'best decisions' in your organisation? Do people have time and space to generate the best ideas? Do they have access to information and expertise? Does the culture support people taking this kind of initiative? Who is making the decisions? Is it the right people? What criteria do people use to make those decisions? Do those decisions take the organisation towards the mission or purpose and are they in alignment with the ethos of the organisation or not?

As you start to ask these questions, other people will start as well. This is the multiplier effect of leadership. Your curiosity not only leads to better ideas and better decision-making, but to deeper curiosity and a willingness by others to move towards tensions. Your leadership creates more leadership rather than more followership.

'Best work' also means embracing the humanity of humans

Ultimately, people can't do their best work in an inhumane environment. Can people bring their humanity to serve the bigger purpose or mission? If they can't, you aren't getting their best.

If people can't bring their humanity, it means that better ideas, better solutions and better implementation are out there somewhere, but outside of your grasp. If you're getting 60% of what people have to offer because they are unable to bring their whole selves to work, you're not getting their best contribution.

Does the physical environment in which people work enable them to bring their full humanity?

Does the psychological environment enable people to bring their full humanity? Is it safe to be themselves? Is difference valued? Does the organisation embrace emotion? Are people treated humanely or like second-rate machines? Can people connect with themselves, with each other, with the customer or client? Can they afford to care?

We've never really dedicated ourselves to creating this kind of environment and therefore we've never really needed leaders to care about the *humane-ity* of the environment. We've never really needed leaders who were tuned in to whether the environment was humane. In a leader's back pocket were always the tools to control. The leader was always able to say, 'If needs be, I can just *make* this happen. Because I am the boss.'

There will be situations where, not because you are the boss but because you have decision-making authority in a particular situation (because of a role you have in the organisation), you will be the one to make a final call. But the authority to make a decision isn't bound up with leadership. It is a separate authority that comes from your expertise or your experience. As we saw in Chapter 3, decision-making authority doesn't have to sit with the 'boss'. There doesn't even need to be a boss. It can be distributed to the best person or people to make that decision. Sometimes that will be you, but it isn't you simply by virtue of your role. A leader's authority doesn't come from a job title or positional power. *Leadership is in the eye of the beholder.* You are only a leader if others see you as such.

This doesn't sound like leadership

Our conventional ideas about leadership are based on a leader-follower model. You're not leading unless others are following, so the type of leadership I've described here might not sound like leadership. It might sound like a glorified coach or facilitator, enabling others and their talent, but not leading.

Two critical elements make this leadership.

The first is that you are standing on the horizon, waving the beacon. You are creating that tension between 'what is' and 'what could be'. In that way, you are directing people's attention to the future and creating, like a taut elastic band, a pull towards something better. Rather than people blindly following you, in a rather passive way, with a 'Sure, whatever you say, boss' attitude, they take themselves on the journey.

For this to work, the beacon you're waving has to be meaningful to others. It has to be 'worth it' for them. They aren't going there because you said so. They are going there because it matters to them to go there. This is something we will talk about in the next chapter.

Inherent in the concept of leadership is 'change'. Leadership isn't required when you are staying put. Management is about working within 'what is'. It is about maintaining the status quo. Change requires leadership. Without leadership, there is no shared direction, no shared destination and no shared sense of purpose. People are not going to go through the inevitable pain of change without this.

The second element that makes this leadership is that 'you go first'. Whatever you are asking others to do, you need to do it first:

- Will others need to change? Then you need to change first.

- Will others need to be more understanding of your perspective? Then you need to be more understanding of theirs first.

- Will others need to use new technology? Then you need to use new technology (it has to be new to you, not tech you're used to even if that tech will be new to them).

- Will others need to take care of their well-being? Then you need to take care of your well-being.

- Will others need to speak openly and honestly? Then you will need to speak openly and honestly.

- Will others have to let go of old beliefs and ways of working? Then you will need to let go of old beliefs and ways of working.

You are clearing a path. Think of it like an overgrown jungle. You are slashing away the undergrowth to make space for others to walk more freely. You do that by doing whatever you are asking them to do yourself, first. If you are not experiencing the pain of change, how can you expect them to?

Going first not only clears the path, but it is a learning opportunity for you. I recall working with a team that agreed to implement a hybrid and flexible working policy in their organisation. I suggested they try it first, but they worried that, if they attempted to work flexibly, it would look like they weren't committed to the company, like they were just seeking an excuse to slack off.

The issues that were coming up for them were the exact issues that would come up for other teams. They wanted others to do something, to take a risk, to embrace a change and sit with the discomfort of that change, even though they were not willing to do so themselves.

The same happens when a team tells me that other teams in the organisation aren't listening to them. When I ask, 'Are you listening as deeply and with as open a mind as you expect them to listen to you?' they shift uncomfortably in their seats. They want to be listened to, but they don't want to listen.

Leadership is about experiencing the discomfort first so you can empathise with others as they experience the same barriers later. It's about experiencing the barriers first so you can develop some strategies and insights that might help others overcome them later. It's about experiencing the pain of change so that you, with credibility from your lived experience, can hold others' feet to the fire when necessary, knowing you got through the pain and came out the other side, and they can too.

The difference between a team and a working group

What about all the other stuff? The bundle of responsibilities that you assumed when you started managing people? Have I described an idealistic situation where you get to float around all day looking for tensions and facilitating thought-provoking discussions with colleagues?

Firstly, I don't believe this is an ideal. It is how leaders need to lead today to bring about a radical reformation in how we work, for the benefit of the people in our organisations (their sense of meaning, purpose, desire to do a great job, development of their talent, well-being), for the benefit of our organisations (to enable them to deliver on their mission or purpose in service of their customers, clients and the wider community), and to adapt to a different context (advances in technology, the health of the planet, constant disruption in every industry, the sheer pace of change) than the context which gave us the original rules of work in the first place.

Secondly, what I've described isn't necessarily a full-time role. It's the role you're performing when you are leading. The rest of the time you may have other roles as a technical expert, or as a mentor, or as a contributor on a working group or as a manager.

At this stage, it's important to differentiate between a manager and a leader and between a team and a working group.

You may think you manage a team. Most likely you manage a working group.

The differences between a team and a working group are clearly described in a classic *Harvard Business Review* article from 1993, 'The Discipline of Teams'.[39] Working groups have a strong, clearly focused leader (or, in fact, *manager* by my definition). Individuals in the working group have individual accountability and work on individual work products. The working group comes together in efficient meetings, sharing its purpose with the broader organisational mission. There are discussions and decisions, and then activity is delegated.

For instance, an HR working group might consist of an HR director and then several other HR professionals – business partners, specialists in some aspect of HR like organisational development, learning, admin etc. The members of that working group come together for meetings to update the HR director and each other about what they are working on and to discuss topics where the input of others might be helpful. Then they go off and do their jobs. They may spend most of their time with other departments or with subgroups of their main working group.

We refer to this group as a team, but it isn't.

Teams, by Katzenbach and Smith's definition, have a specific, shared purpose for which they are all *collectively* accountable. They share the leadership of that team. Performance is measured by assessing the collective work they have produced, not the individuals' contributions. They discuss, debate and decide together. I would refine that last point a little by saying that they discuss and debate, but decision-making may be distributed depending on who in the team is best placed to make the final call. Coming to a joint decision is problematic and tends to lead to either bland, meaningless decisions, or 'fake' decisions where the majority wins but not everyone agrees.

Teams don't need managers. They don't have a hierarchy in that sense. However, they will certainly need leadership of the kind described in this chapter. Teams may form because a tension has been noticed and there is enthusiasm for addressing it. The best people to address that tension are brought together. Each brings something unique to the team – expertise, thinking style, talent – and together they work on the problem.

The role of the leader (or leaders) is different to the role of the manager.

When someone is made a manager these days, they take on board a huge bundle of responsibilities which are rarely defined. These include:

- Developing their people

- Planning their objectives, including their development objectives

- Delegating to them and then keeping an eye on their progress

- Providing them with feedback, coaching, wise counsel, and a shoulder to cry on

- Checking how they are doing on a personal level

- Critiquing their direct reports' work and adding expertise

- Regular 1-2-1s, social events, lunches, check ins on a less formal basis

- Wandering about and asking people about their weekend

- Taking issues their people can't resolve and resolving them or escalating them

- Communicating messages from above, whether they believe in the decision or not

- Being available to their direct reports whenever needed

- Resolving conflict

- Knowing some of the basics of HR law so they don't accidentally put their foot in it

- Running meetings

- Reading reports their people have written to stay informed

- Being cc'd on emails that are 'of interest'

- Modeling the values of the organisation

- Modeling the leadership behaviours of the organisation

- Deciding who gets a promotion, a pay rise or a bonus

- Thanking and appreciating people

- Being accessible to junior people so as not to seem distant and aloof

- Being part of a team (or working group) of peers

- Representing their function

- Advocating for their function to secure their profile, budget and resources

- Supporting their peers and trying not to seem like they care about their own function more than they care about theirs

- Hiring and firing

- Onboarding new people

- Being a leader beyond the day-to-day management, which might include leading other initiatives outside of their management remit

- Staying up to date with industry trends, networking and connecting with clients

- Being brought out as a 'Big Gun' when needed

What have I missed out?

No wonder you are so busy and spread so thin – and this is on top of your own 'work'. Very rarely do organisations create managers who solely spend their days managing others. You have deliverables, too.

We've already covered the reasons so much of this activity exists in previous chapters. I'd encourage you to go through this list and consider how much of it relates to those Victorian beliefs (people can't be trusted, people are second-rate machines) and consider whether working on trust and your attachment to the hierarchy could liberate you from much of this busy-work.

Pushing decision-making down, giving away your authority, treating people like they want to do a great job instead of managing people as if they are trying to get away with something and, as described earlier in this chapter, getting curious about the tensions in the system that obstruct them from doing their best work, should free you up from a great deal of things on this list.

You could also go through this list and categorise the types of work into different role 'labels'. Rather than a bundle of activities entitled 'manager', can these activities be subdivided in other ways? Which of these activities sit under the heading of 'mentoring'? Which of these activities are pastoral care or even 'parenting'? Which of these come under the heading 'technical expert'? Which justifiably can be described as 'leadership'?

A distinction I make between management and leadership is around 'scale'. A manager might be interested in the well-being of an individual. That's where the pastoral care comes in. You notice someone in your team is under stress, tired or in conflict with a client or colleague. As a manager, you want to help, so you create time for them, listening, coaching, giving advice, stepping in and fixing the problem. This covers a lot of the activity on the list above.

A leader, however, while they care on a human level for someone else's distress, is looking at tensions in the system for the solution, rather than the presenting issue. They aren't focused on the situation but on the root cause of the situation, and a sustainable solution.

Here's an example:

Management: Let's say someone you manage is struggling with a particularly difficult client. You, as their manager, may arrange a 1-2-1, spending time advising them on how to deal with difficult clients, and sharing your experience as a mentor or as wise counsel. You may join your more junior colleague in meetings with the difficult client acting as a buffer, modeling how to handle such situations or being the 'Big Gun' that puts an end to the silliness (while you are in the room, at least). You may move that individual off that client and put someone else in their place with more experience or with a different personality. Or you may escalate the situation to your own manager, a 'Bigger Gun', to have words with the client and defuse the situation. For now.

Leadership: In the same situation, you, as a leader, will look for where the tension truly lies. Is this situation unique to this colleague and this specific client? Or is this something that comes up quite frequently as an issue between 'us' and 'them'? Chances are, it comes up quite frequently. So frequently, in fact, that managers are often brought in to sort these situations out, and a great deal of learning and development time goes into arming employees with the skills to handle difficult clients. Meditation and wellness days are organised to help employees cope with the stress of difficult clients, and employees occasionally take time off because they are burnt out meaning others have to cover their workload, which creates more strain on everyone.

The leader is curious about the systemic issue. Is it how we contract with clients? Is it the kinds of clients we work with? Is it down to how we position ourselves in the market and therefore the sorts of clients we attract? Is it the way we work with those clients, how connections and relationships are made and nurtured? Is it about a clash of values or ethos between us and the clients? Is it our willingness to tolerate certain behaviours early on in the relationship? Is it about how we price ourselves? Is it about the types of employees we need versus those we are willing to pay for? Is it about the quality of work we produce? Is it about how well we listen to clients' needs or what we promise at the point of sale? Is it because we care more about our top line than our bottom line? Is it because we'd rather look 'big' even though it makes it hard to be profitable, rather than 'small' with healthier margins? Or something else?

If we assume that most people are trying to do a good job, most people care and most people aren't trying to get away with something, this applies just as much to the people we interact with client-side as it does our employees. What is really going on here, time and time again?

Leaders are looking systemically while managers are dealing with the presenting issue.

Managers make the most of the status quo. Leaders look at what is, and what could be, and disrupt the status quo to bring about change to make things better, permanently.

I've known businesses completely rethink the kinds of clients they are willing to work with, how much they will charge for their services, how they will onboard clients, what kinds of people they need in their business and how their ethos will drive how they collaborate with clients rather than doing whatever they are asked by the client because of, you know, the money.

In the short term, they have often paid a price – normally, financial – for these choices. They contracted in size because they've fired clients. They've had to let people go. They've reorganised and rethought their recruitment and client acquisition strategies, and they've come back stronger than before, with ethos at the heart of everything they do.

That's leadership.

Let's get real

In most organisations today there is an expectation that you will do the management. Saying that, you probably have more freedom to do it your own way than you think. Is anyone checking?

How about your 'team' meetings – do they have to be working group meetings or could you become a true team and just not shout about it... yet?

How about the various projects and initiatives you've been assigned to 'lead' which you are currently 'managing'? Could you rethink those and show up as a leader instead, creating a team that looks and acts quite differently to the norms in your organisation, breaking some 'rules' of behaviour, structure and decision-making? Does anyone have to know?

In this way, you can start to experience what leadership looks like, what it feels like and what comes up for you as you adopt this approach, without drawing attention to yourself, just yet.

As Chris May described in my interview with him, it requires effort and continual attention, personal growth and self-awareness to shift away from conventional management approaches and the myths of leadership to the kind of leader he needs to be for his organisation and the people within it to thrive. The same will be true for you. You will fail. You will give in to the temptation to tell people what to do. You will get distracted by the suffering of individuals and forget to look for the systemic causes. Then you will remember what you were trying to do and have another go.

Equally, the people in these new types of 'teams' you create will be confused. They will try to get you to tell them what to do. They will try to get you to step in and fix situations for them. They will tell you they need more 1-2-1 time with you. They will defer to you and your 'wisdom' because that's what they've been trained to do. They will make mistakes. They will tell you this new way isn't working.

Then, over time, the re-wiring will occur. Yours and theirs. They will find taking ownership rewarding. They will start to trust that you mean it when you say they are in charge, not you. They will become curious, start asking better questions and seeking out tensions to resolve, and you will have less and less busy-work in your diary. There will be more time to think, to debate, to get creative, to anticipate what lies ahead rather than constant firefighting. You will have more time to lead.

And the rest of the organisation will start to notice. Things will start to change.

Action 4: Question everything at a systemic level

In every system there are tensions, things that don't quite work. Often, we find workarounds, or we wait until the system is so broken that we need a huge transformation programme that changes everything at once. This transformation often creates new tensions, which we tolerate and work around until it becomes too much, at which point we do a huge transformation again.

For an organisation to withstand constant disruption and uncertainty, it needs to be willing to constantly adapt, flex and change. This means the job of a leader is to look for tensions, go towards them and fix them (or engage others in fixing them). They do this knowing that new tensions will arise as a result, and they will go towards those, too.

It is the willingness to constantly ask questions that reveal the systemic tensions which dominate the mind of a leader. So, when you are leading, it's your willingness to question everything which comes to the fore.

Leaders don't just accept that the way we work, the way we serve customers and clients, the industry we're in, the norms of that industry and the norms of our profession are written in stone. They recognise that these norms were invented by other human beings and can, therefore, change.

Leaders may lead the thinking, but they don't always make the changes by themselves. By asking challenging questions and prompting people to think differently about the present and the future, they create space for others to grasp the opportunity. Their questioning is contagious. They are patient zero – they lead the asking of the questions.

To lead, you have to look closely at habitual thinking, conventional wisdom, industry norms and everything we take for granted, and question them – 'Really? Is that a fact? Does it have to be that way? What if we rejected that? Is it true? What else might be true?'

This question – is it true? – is one of my favourites. It comes from American speaker and author Byron Katie.[40]

What is true? Just because we believe it, does that make it true? Just because our society is built on this belief, does that make it true? What if it isn't true? What if something else is just as true, or more true? How does believing what we believe to be true serve us, and how does it limit us?

Is it true that people need to be managed? Is it true that people need to get permission to spend a budget? Is it true that you are meant to have the answers? Is it true that people are resistant to change? Is it true that some people lack motivation? Is it true…?

Questioning everything means questioning the most sacred of 'truths' about your organisation, your people, technology, your industry and the world. AI doesn't question. It isn't curious. It can problem-solve, for sure, and it can sift data, but AI couldn't write this book because it doesn't have an opinion. It can only condense other people's opinions. Originality comes from the ability to ask questions that other people aren't asking. Leaders are leaders because they are leading the asking of questions.

How do you feel about this? If you're honest with yourself, are you a little scared?

If you believe that people are second-rate machines who can't be trusted to think for themselves, and if you believe people are trying to take the organisation for a ride and need tight controls, you simply won't lead in the way I've described. It will be too great a risk.

But, in a world where technology can do what technology does best – nonemotional, data-driven tasks and decisions – human beings can be used to ask questions that, perhaps, they didn't have time to ask before. By delegating to the nonhuman workforce, we have the opportunity to liberate our human workforce in a way we've never been able to before. Their human potential has always been curtailed until now.

If we could get away from our computers, stop all the hours of writing and presenting reports, hand over to technology the planning and organising of people and things, slash the hours spent in waste-of-time meetings, do away with time-consuming workarounds of systems, processes and tech that doesn't work the way it's supposed to, and anything else that slowly kills your soul at work, we would have time and space to question and think and create and connect... all the qualities unique to human beings. That is how we will allow people to do their best work in pursuit of the mission and purpose of the organisation.

You're a leader in this reformation if you are willing to go first – to start asking questions. Are you up for that?

LISTEN NOW

Diederick Janse is a Holacracy Master Coach and trainer, and a partner at Energized (https://energized. org/en/what-we-do), which supports organisations to move towards self-management. Holacracy is a particular form of self-management about which you can learn more at www.holacracy.org. In this conversation, Diederick and I discuss self-management in more depth but with a focus on leadership and what he refers to as 'citizenship within organisations'.

You can listen to the interview at **www. buzzsprout.com/2250059/13671828** or listen to any of the other interviews here: **https:// punksinsuitshowtoleadtheworkplacereformation. buzzsprout.com**

Summary

To bring about radical reformation in how we work and how we create organisations that can thrive in fast-changing, uncertain times, we need leaders who prioritise creating environments in which people can do their best work in pursuit of the mission or purpose of the organisation. Most organisations are riddled with tensions that are worked around, creating extra work, conflict, inefficiency and suboptimal outcomes for clients and customers, as well as perpetuating highly dysfunctional cultures that prevent people from bringing everything they have to offer as human beings.

You have to become the caretaker of the organisation's mission, purpose and ethos, waving a beacon to show people where they are heading and why it matters. You need to go towards tensions. At all times you are asking what gets in the way of people doing their best work. What gets in the way of their talent? What gets in the way of the best decisions?

At the same time, you need to shed as much of the management work as you dare. Turning working groups into teams, distributing authority and decision-making, treating people with trust and focusing not on individual suffering but systemic causes of suffering will, eventually, change how much time you have to actually lead, and how willing others around you will be to adopt a leadership mindset themselves – getting curious, going towards tensions and asking big questions.

Questions to consider

- Why do we do it that way?
- What are the benefits of doing it that way?
- How does doing it that way limit us?
- Which vested interests are served by doing it that way?
- What outdated beliefs underpin doing it that way?
- What if we didn't do it that way?
- What is suboptimal in how we organise people and things?
- What barriers are there to doing our best work?
- What prevents people from bringing their whole value to their job here?
- How do I get in the way?

- What do we constantly work around or tolerate?

- What is harder than it needs to be?

- What drains us when it should inspire us?

- What processes cause friction between people and teams?

- What annoys our clients?

- Where do we compromise our values or our ethos?

CHAPTER 5

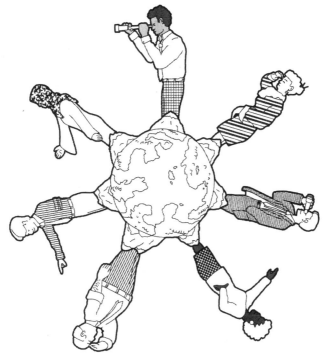

change

Change
Talkin' 'Bout A Reformation

A few years ago, I was coaching a leadership team as they endeavoured to change the culture of their organisation. They saw that, much as I have described so far in this book, people were doing great work *despite* the culture, the structure and the processes that had been hardwired into the organisation over time. If you don't actively look for tensions and address them in real time you will find yourself deepening them and the workarounds required to navigate them, and, eventually, you will need a root-and-branch rethink of everything all at once. Most major organisational change projects are like this.

That leadership team realised that their structure was part of the problem. This isn't my area, so we brought in experts to help them think scientifically about alternatives. At the start of the process, they identified the success criteria for the new structure. If it was to be better than the current structure, what problems would need to be addressed? For them, being customer-centric was crucial. They wanted their customers' experience to be simple and efficient.

The consultants helped them generate five or six alternative structures to the one they already had. The current structure, changing nothing, was also an option.

Over the course of two days, they analysed all the options against the success criteria that they had identified.

At the end of the process, one option was by far the most suitable, meeting almost all the success criteria. While there is no perfect structure (every structure has strengths and weaknesses), this one – Option C – was the best.

But one member of the team was unhappy. Let's call him Lars.

Lars wanted to review the process, to go back to the start, to rethink the success criteria and the options and do the scoring again. His colleagues were shocked. He had played an active part in the whole two-day process. He had spoken openly throughout, fully engaging and influencing the outcome, yet he didn't like the result.

What was his problem?

His colleagues got curious, asking him what he was unhappy about and where he thought the logical process had been flawed. It turned out, as they gently questioned him (where they got the patience, I do not know!), that he thought his new team would be smaller in the new structure. He didn't openly say this was the reason for his objection, it just came out.

His colleagues explained that, in fact, his team would be bigger in the new structure. He took a moment, thoughtfully stroking his chin and, staring up at the matrix of options on the wall, declared that maybe, after all, Option C could work well.

Busting the myths of change

Inherent in the definition of leadership is the concept of change. You don't need leadership if you aren't changing anything. Maintaining the status quo is what management is all about, but change requires leadership of the kind I've described because it needs someone to wave the beacon on the horizon, reminding people of the direction of travel, and it needs someone to clear a path, identifying – or enabling others to identify – tensions which stop people doing their best in pursuit of that destination.

If you are to leave things better than they are today, something (many things) will need to change.

However, we are stuck with some outdated notions of change. These notions, if they were ever true, aren't true today. They are the reason efforts to change organisations rarely achieve the original ambitions. In the process, the ideal is diluted to make it palatable and easier to implement, damage is done to levels of trust because change is 'forced', and it can take years to unpick the baggage, during which time more change is due, already being built on weak foundations.

So often I've been brought in to help a culture heal from the last big disruption in order to get it ready for the next one. The thinking is that everyone needs to be in good shape before the upheaval begins again so they can tolerate the mess that's about to hit the fan. This process of breaking relationships in order to drive change, then attempting to rebuild them so they can withstand being broken again, is not sustainable, particularly given that, these days, there is no longer a time when nothing is changing, and therefore there is never enough time to heal before going again.

In this chapter, I'm going to bust three myths about change so that, as you consider how to embrace the ideas in this book, you can go about change without hurting relationships with the very people you are trying to liberate.

Myth 1: Change is logical

It is a deeply held belief that people don't like change. After all, they make a big fuss about it, don't they? Typically, any change has a logical explanation. In the case of Lars, above, the process of agreeing on a way forward was logical. Surely, then, a rational person should have been persuaded?

Except that's not what happened. Despite the logic, Lars couldn't get behind the change for *emotional* reasons. When he eventually bought in, it was because his *emotional* reaction to the change went from negative to positive.

The first myth we have to bust is that change is logical. It isn't. It's emotional.

The myth that people don't like change assumes that people are logical beings, like machines. When a decision makes logical sense but people are resistant to it, we revert to the widely held belief that people don't like change. After all, this change makes total logical sense, so how could anyone be against it? It must be because people don't like change.

When this is our starting point, we assume that any resistance to change is simply human nature. It's our wiring. If you are going to leave your organisation better than it is today, change is inevitable, but unless you understand why people do and do not change, you will be forced to revert to command and control, Victorian-style approaches to change. That will undermine the very change you are trying to bring about.

If what you desire is an empowered, humane environment where people can come and do their best work without so many of the barriers that currently exist, and yet you are going to bring about that new environment by force, you've lost credibility already.

Most change programmes today are, in fact, a dressed-up form of command and control.

It goes like this: you, the leader, know best. You know what is in the best interests of other people. They are going to resist because they don't like change. You are alright with change because you're a superior human. That's why you're a leader. You've tried explaining the 'why' – the logic. No one can argue with the logic. It fixes the very problems they've told you they are experiencing! But, just like Lars, they don't like the logical solution. If they won't come willingly, you'll have to drag them along, convince them it's for their own good, implement the new system/process/tech/structure despite their resistance and, hopefully, once it is in place, they will understand and thank you for making them change.

I'm being facetious. These days, most change is a far more consultative process than I have described. People are asked for their input. A lot of listening goes on. Solutions are often generated with their collaboration. Partnership is valued. Still, because we believe people are inherently resistant to change, when they are true to form and resist, we reassure ourselves that this is inevitable and that we have to plough on. They will be grateful in the end, we tell ourselves, and those who aren't probably shouldn't be part of our future anyway.

If you look at almost all conventional models of change, they have three parts:

1. Identify what change is necessary.

2. Explain and get buy-in.

3. Implement the change and get the results.

The process of bringing about change focuses on logic – what are the problems? Where are the pain points? What are the possible solutions to address those problems and pain points? Which ones most effectively address those problems and pain points? Decision made – let's go.

However, if we accept that change is emotional, not logical, the process has to look rather different. Lars was on board with the logic until his emotions came into play. He didn't want a smaller team. His ego was tied up in having a large team. He wasn't going to tell anyone this was one of the success criteria that mattered to him. He wasn't asked, and even if he had been, he couldn't tell anyone because he didn't know. He specifically told me at the start of day one that he was able to keep his emotions outside the room! Even when it became clear to the rest of us that his objection to Option C was entirely emotional, he didn't recognise it. He still, at that stage, believed the logic was flawed and put his conversion down to having misunderstood the logic until his colleagues re-explained the process they'd been through over the last two days.

What if we turn the belief that people don't like change on its head? What if we start with a belief that people are good at change? The evidence is all around us.

People are good at change

People change jobs. They move house. They start hobbies and projects. They have children. They go on holiday somewhere new. They get divorced. They change careers.

Human beings are highly adaptable. We can reconfigure our lives and our world and have done so throughout our existence. It is why we are still here.

When we start with that understanding, resistance to change takes on a new meaning. Perhaps it isn't change per se that people don't like. It's *this* change, done in *this* way. Our emotions are telling us something important. Rather than pushing past them, we need to stop and connect with them. Maybe what our emotions have to say is more important (or at least equally as important) as what logic tells us?

We need a different approach to one based on logic and force. This shift starts – as we explored in previous chapters – with rethinking what a leader is and how they create space for people to do their best work rather than *drive* people to do good work. It means reflecting on our attachment to hierarchy and the ego boost we get from it, which undermines our deeper sense of meaning. Of course, it also means being willing to trust rather than assuming people are trying to get away with something.

That means we have to unpick some of our habits of thinking around change specifically, starting with the idea that logic is our primary tool. Of course, logic needs to inform the solution, but it isn't the only factor. If people aren't emotionally invested in the change, if we haven't created an environment where the emotional journey is as much part of the process as logic, change cannot happen.

You can implement a new system, even a new structure, but for change to be effective people need to change their minds. Read that again – people need to *change their minds*. Change of behaviour is only sustainable when there is a change of mind. Someone can tell me that I need to eat more veg and less cake, and I can know logically this is true, but unless I change the emotional connection I have with cake, I will always reach for it when I'm sad, happy, lonely, stressed, relaxed… Cake is meeting an emotional need which is stronger than logic.

Every human in your organisation operates this way, whether they acknowledge it or not. Some are more aware of their emotional inner world, while others are completely in the dark, like Lars. As a leader intent on bringing about change, you need to put emotion and emotional self-awareness at the heart of change. Perhaps the biggest change your organisation needs is this – prioritising the value of emotion as a tool, rather than seeing it as an obstacle to the successful achievement of the purpose or mission of the organisation.

Emotions are the differentiator

If people aren't second-rate machines but first-rate humans, it is their emotions that are the differentiator. When Lars told me that he could leave his emotions at the door, I thought to myself, 'Well, then a machine could take your place.' If we aren't going to love emotion, of all flavours, then we are saying a machine could do our job.

Emotional self-awareness and comfort with the emotions of others isn't something most of us learn in childhood. It isn't a major part of the school curriculum and, as a society, we haven't prioritised emotional self-awareness either. This could explain why our society is so toxic to our emotional well-being. Even when we focus on our emotional well-being, it is often in an attempt to cope with the onslaught of life, rather than to change anything as a result. We might meditate, work with a therapist, work with a coach, take a resilience course, become a mental-health first-aider, or even take some time off to recover after burnout, and then we dive back into the fray.

One of my motivations for becoming a keynote speaker was that I felt my 1-2-1 coaching was often about patching leaders up only to send them back out into battle. They would arrive at sessions frazzled, broken, exhausted. We would talk. They would decide how to handle a situation differently. Then they'd go back out there, only to return a month later frazzled, broken and exhausted again. When I saw the pattern, I knew I had to change my approach. Instead of working within the system, I needed to talk about fixing the system, getting to the heart of what was breaking my clients and finding the root cause. We have to see all these emotions as a signal – a vital signal – for the need to change, as change guru Cassandra Worthy says in my interview with her (at the end of this chapter).

This is as true for you as it is for others. Your emotions are just as much a factor in your willingness to change as anyone else.

If I may tell another story…

A few years ago, I was working with a leadership team as they endeavoured to change the culture of their organisation. This is a different team. Don't be too surprised. This is pretty much what I do for a living, and then I talk about it on stage.

The team was made up of directors from three different legacy businesses. Following the merger of these three businesses, they were attempting to create one new culture which took the best from all three. However, some of the directors were finding change much easier than others. Why, they asked, were some of the team so resistant?

Because not everyone in the team was required to change to the same degree. Those who were finding change the hardest were those whose ways of working, ways of thinking and fundamental beliefs, would need to change the most for the three cultures to come together as something new. Those who were finding change easiest had the least amount of change to go through.

The new united culture was not that different to the one they'd had before the merger. Taking the best from each of the three legacy businesses didn't mean taking the best equally. One of the three was different in ethos – much more old-fashioned, less suited to new approaches to technological innovation, more attached to its long history and less profitable.

The people from that business had the most to do. They had to come face to face with more discomfort. They had to change their minds about fundamentals which had guided their behaviours for decades.

It is easy to look at others and ask why they are finding change so hard when you are finding it so easy, but maybe you have less to change than them.

To have credibility when you talk about change, you need to be willing to change as well. The change you need to confront might not be embracing a new set of organisational values or a new bit of tech. Emotionally, you're already on board with that, but what *do* you need to change your mind about? Is it how you view other people and their struggles? Is it how open you are to their emotions? Is it your willingness to listen and be influenced by how others feel? What emotions are coming up for you and, if these emotions are a signal of the need to change, where do you need to change?

Change is emotional. It should be. As a leader, get comfortable with other people's emotions – of all kinds – and your own. Let them out. Get curious about them. Allow emotion into the conversation. Human beings are good at change, as long as they have the time, the space and the skills to process what is coming up, emotionally.

When to get interested in emotion

A note here: if you wait until it's time to change something before getting interested in how people are, forming relationships or focusing your attention on building trust, it's too late. Most people are not yet highly tuned into their emotions, their beliefs, their inner world... or, if they are, they don't intentionally bring that side of themselves to work. Trying to get them to talk from the heart or observe their inner workings and make meaning of them when you're against the clock trying to introduce a new tech system or restructure your organisation won't be effective.

What you're trying to do here is change the nature of work, not just drive change for a moment in time. That means bringing emotion into the workplace *all the time*. It means creating an environment where people's feelings have relevance. It means taking cues from how people are feeling and using those cues to root out tensions. There is *never* a time where you can say, 'Right, we listened, we tried to understand, you had the opportunity to get that off your chest, now can you just get on with the work, please?'

If people are to do their best work, they have to be healthy. They have to feel they are a human and that their humanity can thrive. This isn't the same as making sure everyone is happy. It is about your personal development and their personal development – people's increased self-awareness of their operating system, why certain emotions come up, how to explore those emotions and how to grow as a result.

Leadership development is personal development. The limits on the quality of your leadership are personal development limits. If you don't grow as a person and become more attuned to why you do what you do, why you think as you do and how you get in your way, you won't become a better leader. Part of this personal development is developing others, helping them become more attuned to themselves and their inner world.

Humans have a rich and fascinating inner world. We owe it to them to unpick 250 years of Industrial-Age beliefs that most people are basic, uninteresting, unthinking machines who just want to be told what to do and then go home.

One day, perhaps, people will come into the working world without these beliefs, and already aware of the skills and priorities I have been talking about in this chapter – if our education system and our society catch up and recognise the need for this. Until then, most people won't do this work on themselves until they join the workforce. Their personal growth is now your business.

Myth 2: You can plan for change

In 2018 my then ten-year-old daughter and I, along with our two dogs, set off on a seven-month 'digital nomad' adventure. We sold our house, bought a campervan and travelled around Europe, staying at Airbnbs if we were going to be in one place for a while, or living out of the van on the road. The purpose of the trip was, in part, to see if it was possible to be location-independent. In other words, well before the pandemic forced so many people to work from home and connect to each other only by the internet, I wanted to see whether it was possible to run a business without having a permanent base.

I also wanted to put myself into a state of change again. Having worked with so many leadership teams, and helping them navigate change, I realised I hadn't experienced much change myself for a while. I realised I couldn't empathise. I had forgotten what the journey of change felt like, and what emotions were likely to come up because I'd been keeping myself rather safe inside my comfort zone.

So off we went.

The first night in the van it snowed. This was March, so we had assumed the worst weather had passed. We were wrong. Huddled inside our campervan, we realised that we hadn't thought things through very well. For one thing, I didn't know how the heater worked because I thought we wouldn't need it. There was also nowhere to sit. We had filled the interior with cushions and throws which looked lovely on Instagram, but were taking up a huge amount of space.

On day one, we bought an electric heater and discarded all the cushions.

For all the planning, following other digital nomads on social media, imagining life on the road and shopping trips for 'essentials', it wasn't until we were living out of the van that we started to understand what we needed, and what we didn't.

This is what I learnt: you can't plan for change. The truth is, 'You won't know until you go.'

Much effort goes into planning for change. In fact, planning and preparation are key to successful change. This is when the consultation happens, when people are asked what problems they are facing and what solutions might make things better. It is when budgets and timeframes are established. It is when 'buy-in' to the principle is prioritised. Everything is prepared for the go-date. If, the thinking goes, we prepare properly, then the launch should be pretty simple. We can even address all of the emotions before we set off so there won't be any objection after.

Except that, until day one *after* launch, you haven't changed anything. Change begins on day one, not before. Everything before day one is wishful thinking. While emotion will come up before then, in anticipation of change, only the experience of change will bring the most visceral emotions to the surface.

I'm not saying don't plan. I'm saying that you won't really know what you're planning for until you start the journey, even if you've done this kind of thing before.

It was only while trying to warm my body in front of the brand-new fan heater, having made a massive pile of all those lovely cushions ready to take them to a nearby charity shop, that I thought, 'What have we done?' To be honest, if I hadn't handed the keys to our house to the estate agent the day before, I would have gone back home. That was when the real significance of what we'd done, the scale of the risk, the uncertainty, and how little I knew, came into sharp focus.

By trying to 'manage' change in a business, we attempt to minimise the discomfort, but the neat models of change often skip over the stage between planning and results. They call this stage 'Implement Change', as if that's the easy bit.

Taking a bug-fix approach

In fact, 'Implement Change' isn't one stage at all. In his book *Leadership Is Language*, David Marquet shares the story of a ship called El Faro and the tragic loss of all on board.[41] I highly recommend you read it. A major theme of the book is our tendency to make a leadership decision in advance of a journey, and then stick to that decision despite new information coming to light along the way. Hierarchy made it difficult or impossible for the crew of El Faro to question the decisions of the captain, and the captain did not want to be seen as weak (or to imply his crew were not capable) by changing his mind, even as the weather conditions worsened.

This is the problem with a highly detailed plan. We make the plan with the information we have before embarking on the journey. We base that plan on previous experience, but we also create a plan that is meant to reassure. We want our bosses to be reassured that we have thought things through, that we have considered the risks and minimised them. Our bosses don't want chaos. They want machine-like predictability before they will allow us to go ahead, so we try to give them that.

We also create a plan that won't scare the people. 'People don't like change', we tell ourselves, so we present a plan that reassures them this won't be painful, it's totally safe, nothing to worry about, just do what the plan says and nothing bad will happen.

We also create a plan to reassure ourselves. We don't know how we will deal with uncertainty and the unknown. We don't want surprises that, perhaps, we can't handle, so we try to think of everything before it's too late to turn back.

But, as with my first night in the campervan, you won't know until you go. You cannot prepare fully because you are not a fortune-teller. There will be surprises. New information will come to light. People will say they are fine but, when they realise the implications of the change, they will not be fine. The context might change. Your company might lose a major client meaning budgets are under pressure, or the supplier you've partnered with might turn out to be quite tricksy to deal with. Costs might spiral. Timescales might shift.

The more detailed your original plan, the more difficult it will be to adapt. You won't want to lose credibility, disappoint your bosses or confuse people who thought the plan would keep them safe.

This is why I prefer piloting everything, taking an agile approach and bug-fixing. Create a framework based on what you know before you go, but then be willing to pause, reflect, adjust and go again. The journey itself teaches you. If you are too attached to the plan, you can't learn from the journey and do better.

When we embarked on our digital nomad adventure, I thought I knew what I would learn and how I would grow. I thought I knew the ways I would be different when we returned – I did not. I had to let go of everything I thought I would learn and learn the real lessons of the journey. Those lessons were far more profound than I could have anticipated, but they were also far more painful than I expected. Had I known the pain ahead, I might not have gone in the first place.

This is important – the journey of change will be painful. There is nothing you can do to prevent that. You have to trust yourself and those around you to have the tools and the wherewithal to face that pain, learn lessons, and go again in the light of what you've learnt. You have to hold lightly to the plan and be willing to tweak, refine or totally rethink it along the way.

Myth 3: We are all in this together

How many times have you or another leader issued the rallying cry 'We are all in this together'? It's meant to be inspiring. It's meant to create a sense of unity, of team, of community.

Except you're not all in this together. Every person is going on their own personal, unique journey.

This is especially true when the person issuing the rallying cry is more senior than the audience. Change is like a train going through a tunnel. Some people are at the front of the train. They go into the tunnel first but they also emerge into the light while others, further back, are plunged into darkness.

In a conventional hierarchy, the more senior you are the more influence you have over the decision to change something. You have time to reflect on the options, consider the pros and cons and choose the way forward. Even if you weren't at the table, you were told pretty early on and had time to digest it. Maybe you had access to information that showed you the thinking process of your senior colleagues and the various moving parts that went into the decision.

As information cascades down the business, it gets simplified. Detail is left out and the chance to influence the decision is reduced.

You had time to get your head around it months before the people you are now telling, so when you say, 'We're all in this together' and they are just hearing about the proposals for the first time, that clearly isn't the case. They are just heading into the darkness.

Busting this myth is more than a warning not to use the phrase 'We are all in this together'. It's about recognising that change is a unique and personal experience.

The '10% terrorists' theory

There is a well-worn cliché about people's reaction to change. It is said that 10% of people will be enthusiastic about change, 80% will go along with it, and 10% will be terrorists, actively undermining it.

This is worth questioning (as it is worth questioning all conventional wisdom).

As we've already seen, people change things in their own lives, so if there is resistance to change, it's worth getting curious. Something is coming up for them that is important.

The 10% (if we accept the ratios) who are enthusiastic could be enthusiastic because they are naïve about what lies ahead, like me with the digital nomad adventure. Of course they are on board. They have no idea about the pain coming their way.

The 10% who are 'terrorists' could be those who clearly understand the scale of what's being proposed and what it means. They might not be resistant because they dislike change, but because they have really listened and are visualising more clearly the challenge ahead.

When we assume there will be 10% terrorists, we marginalise people who are hard to reach, seeing them as inevitable casualties of change, but what if we went towards them? What if they became hugely important to our understanding of the change? What if they were our secret weapon? We've talked about going towards tensions previously. Here is another opportunity.

As for the 10% who are enthusiasts... take care of them. Don't take them for granted. When they hit the first bump in the road, a bump they had not anticipated as they went blindly on the journey all enthusiastic and gung-ho, they may become disillusioned. Suddenly the reality hits home.

Even if their enthusiasm wasn't naivety, they still need to be looked after. These are the people who will clear the path, go into the darkness before other people and experience the pain of change early. They can easily become burnt out, feel put upon and that they are carrying an unfair load. Their energy needs to be managed and they need safe places to talk about how they feel and work out how to sustain their commitment.

One of the lessons I learnt on my digital nomad adventure was that 'if you're alone, you'll go home'. There were many times during the seven months we were away that I wanted to give up. Having a community of friends and supporters around me (my team, coaching clients, friends) helped me through. Being able to confess my misgivings, share my struggles and work through my next steps was essential.

Creating opportunities for this in your organisation is essential, too. At different times different people will need these spaces. Sometimes the person who will need these spaces the most will be you.

Action 5: Listen so hard you might change your mind

This is the Wild West, folks. What we are trying to do in our organisations has never been tried before. We are reinventing work and the role that business plays in the world. We are disconnecting from 250 years of Industrial-Age hardwiring and rethinking the role of people in delivering our company's mission or purpose. How can there be a right way to do this?

Certainly, no one person – you – can know the right thing to do.

You need all the brains in your organisation, and all the hearts, too. You need to let go of having the right answers and, instead, ask better questions.

Then you need to listen. You need to listen really hard. You need to listen to what you don't want to hear. More than that, you need to listen so hard that *you might change your mind.*

I'm sure you've been on plenty of training courses where you've been taught how to listen. Maybe it was a coaching course where listening was a way to access the wisdom of the coachee. Maybe it was a course about active listening where you learnt to show in your body language and your words that you had really heard the other person. Maybe you know that it's rude to interrupt, so you pretend to listen by letting the other person finish speaking before telling them what you were going to tell them anyway. Maybe it was a negotiation and influencing course during which you learnt to listen to find weaknesses in the other person's perspective or how to sell your idea to them in a way that made them feel their needs had been taken into account.

But there is another way to listen, and that is to listen so hard that *you* might change your mind.

You have to be willing to change your mind.

Change, as we've seen, is uncertain and unpredictable, and any proposed solution is untested and unknown and no one person can know the right answer.

Think of it like this.

You are standing on top of a mountain. You can see everything in all directions from up here. You think you have the full picture. You are in the best position to make a decision.

But someone else is standing on top of a different mountain. They also think they can see everything from up there, but they have a slightly different angle than you. That's why, to them, the world looks so different and the solution they propose is different to yours.

Typically, we try to convince people to come and stand on our mountain, to see things from where we stand and to admit that our solution is the right one. Instead, you need to go and stand on their mountain. What does it look like from over there? Chances are, you will see why they feel as they do and why your proposal isn't going to work for them.

Having been willing to go and stand on their mountain and acknowledge that you didn't see their point of view until that moment, and that you now see things differently, you can invite them to join you on yours. They may be willing to do that now, and when they do, they will see how different things look from your mountain.

Now, together, you can work out a way forward.

This is *changing your mind*. People see things differently because they are standing in a different place. Go and join them there. If you had their experiences, their perspectives, their personality, you would see things as they do, and that's why there are hundreds or thousands of perspectives in your organisation. Your way – even though it seems obviously right to you – is only your way because of where you're standing.

Embrace the notion that you are not better than other people, you simply have different information. That information might come from experiences you've gathered, or from access to data they don't have because they are more junior than you. It might be because of the way your brain works that you see things differently.

Your job now is to share what you know and listen to what they know, putting all this information on the table to enhance everyone's ability to make a good decision. With that, you need to be 'convincible'.

The old-fashioned approach is that the senior person's job is to 'take people with them'. In other words, to convince the junior people that their decision is the right one. When we talk about 'getting buy-in' or 'alignment', what we mean is that we expect junior people to become convinced that what they've been told to do is right. We expect them to do what we say. If they disagree initially, we expect them to change their mind.

If we do that, though, aren't we asking them to do something we aren't willing to do ourselves? We are asking them to have the capability to change their mind but we are not willing to do the same.

Changing your mind is an inherent part of the future of leadership. Everyone has to be open to being wrong… or, at least, not being right. People at all levels have to hold lightly to their opinions and be willing to see other perspectives. You have to let go of being right.

Who do you find difficult to hear? Whose perspective do you find most challenging? Who is hard to reach? Listen to them so hard you might change your mind.

LISTEN NOW

Cassandra Worthy is a fellow keynote speaker who believes that we can use our emotions as a way to understand our responses to change, and then grow through that change rather than resisting and struggling against it. Her company, Change Enthusiasm Global, helps organisations build resilience and readiness for change. (Find out more at https://changeenthusiasmglobal.com.)

In this conversation, we look at what this means and how you can use your emotions – and help others to do the same – as an invaluable tool in a business environment that is always changing.

You can listen to the interview at **www.buzzsprout.com/2250059/13677620**, or listen to any of the other interviews here: **https://punksinsuitshowtoleadtheworkplacereformation.buzzsprout.com**

Summary

The myths about change ensure that our attempts to change things in our organisations are only ever marginally successful and cause damage to the health of the culture. Given that change is inherent in the concept of leadership, it is vital we reject these myths and replace them with more useful approaches.

Learning to bring emotions into the organisation is essential if change is to be an ongoing, sustainable and healthy process.

Human beings are emotional – that is their differentiator – so it doesn't make sense to keep emotion out of the room. Being willing to pilot, take an agile approach and bug-fix as you go, makes much more sense than rigidly following a mechanical plan which leaves no space for learning or adapting to new information along the way. That means you need to be willing to change your mind, to stand on someone else's mountain and see what the view looks like from there. You aren't all in this together even when you are all heading in the same direction. Change is not a plan with an implementation phase, but an ongoing process through which we grow.

Questions to consider

- What do I tell myself about change that might not be true?

- What do I tell myself about other people that might not be true?

- What emotions are coming up for me and what might they mean?

- How am I getting in my own way?

- How do other people's emotions make me feel?

- What emotions am I uncomfortable with?

- Where am I forcing change? What could I do differently?

- How attached am I to the plan? What do I need to let go of?

- Who does the plan serve? Is it healthy or realistic?

- Am I trying to control the uncontrollable and predict the unpredictable? What if I held more lightly to this?

- Where am I on the journey? Where are others?

- Who do I need to listen to?

- Who do I find it hard to listen to?

- Who is telling me what I don't want to hear?

- Who is hard to reach? How can I hear them better?

- What 'truth' do I need to let go of? Where could I be wrong?

- Am I expecting others to stand on my mountain before standing on theirs?

- Am I really standing on theirs or just biding time until they come to mine?

CHAPTER 6
A FORCE FOR GOOD

A Force For Good
Goody Two Shoes

For at least a decade (if not more) I've been predicting that a dramatically different approach to how we capitalise on the value of the people in our businesses is required. I've presented this as important in my keynotes and in my consultancy work with clients, both because employee expectations have been changing and because our expectations of those employees have been changing.

I've presented a more humane, connected, less ego-centric approach to leadership which is intended to create an environment where people can do their best work without all the barriers and obstacles that make work frustrating.

I've also acknowledged that there was time. I've asked audiences to reflect on one thing they could do differently, a question they could ask such as 'What are the limits I put on my willingness to trust?' and then take that question into their work the next day. I've been relatively laid back, accepting that some leaders will embrace what I'm talking about, and others won't. I've presented a more dramatic change as something over the horizon, rather than here and now. There was time to take small steps and to iterate.

There isn't time now.

We now have a perfect storm which could threaten even the most stable business.

The challenge

Many businesses are already struggling to keep up with their workload. Everything is an emergency. Resources have been cut back to an absolute minimum to keep costs low at a time when prices are spiralling. Systems are creaking and cracks are showing. We have issues around mental health. We have new generations in our businesses with different expectations. We have a generation on boards who talk about empowerment and employee experience but still think it's best practice to retain power and authority (as if you can successfully empower others and still hold on to power yourself). We have a demand for inclusivity and belonging. The climate crisis poses an existential threat, constantly rumbling in the background, as does geopolitical uncertainty which directly or indirectly impacts us all. We have a crisis in trust and concerns about fake news, polarisation and extremism.

Then, as if that wasn't enough, along comes technology that can act like a person but with unlimited mental capacity. People were already being asked to embrace new tech systems, of course, but this tech is something different. It is revolutionary. It makes much of the work currently done by human beings unnecessary. It can solve problems we have been unable to solve. It can handle huge quantities of data and make meaning of it, instantly. It can take instructions and then respond like an assistant, intern or even an industry expert. Some say that we will soon be taking instructions from the tech rather than the other way around.

It is the final straw. It is the catalyst which should be forcing every business leader to face up to the fact that we must urgently rethink the contract we make with our human employees, the kind of work we ask them to do for us, the way we value and reward that contribution, the spaces we create for them to do that inherently human work and the role we, as leaders, play in transforming human work. We must, once and for all, remove the Victorian hardwiring which underpins our organisations and build new concepts which serve today's and tomorrow's world.

For the first time, people strategies and tech strategies need to sit at the centre of our business strategies. In the past, these strategies supported the business's vision. They were in service of the business. Now they *are* the strategy: 'How are we going to use people and technology (human and nonhuman workforce) to solve problems and serve our customers, clients and other stakeholders?'

If you really ask this question, you will realise that a great deal about how you run your business is a barrier to that rather than an enabler. You will realise that people are doing the best they can *despite* the environment, when they should be able to do their best *because* of the environment.

It is now time for you to take a long, hard look at how you ignore, tolerate or condone the status quo. In many ways, it works for you. You have achieved an amount of professional success, authority and power. You have developed skills in navigating – and circumnavigating – the corporate environment. You have mentored others, giving them insight into what it takes to strike the delicate balance between speaking your mind and being invited to the table – too much honesty will get you locked out of important conversations, and too little will mark you out as someone better suited to the lower ranks of the organisation.

The end of your career is on the horizon. If you are a Gen-Xer, you are looking at retirement in the next five to fifteen years. Of course, you may choose to work for longer. Perhaps you'll have to. Perhaps you'll have the chance to get out a little early, but the option is there, at this point, to coast towards the last day, when you hand in your laptop for the final time.

I don't mean to suggest that you won't be working hard. I'm sure you will. You have targets you want to hit, a legacy you want to leave, and a few more mountains to climb, but the time when you had to prove yourself, to pay your dues, to gain the 10,000 hours plus of experience that formed the foundations of your expertise, are done.

I am asking you to risk all of that.

Business has become harder, less profitable, less creative, less fun, less healthy, less enjoyable and less rewarding because we are stuck with an Industrial-Age model that we inherited and which has become hardwired into our psyche, and we are approaching the point where that model is going to be so harmful to our business's viability, and the health of the people within that business, that we *must* do something radical. This is the writing on the wall, and if you can see it, then you must do something differently.

The Generation Game

I've mentioned 'new generations joining the workforce' a few times so far, but I haven't explained what I mean or the implications. As we get close to the end of the book, it's now or never.

I don't want to get carried away with Generation Theory. Ultimately, everyone is an individual and there are many factors affecting a person's values and perspective beyond the decade in which they were born. Making generalisations can be dangerous and stop you from really listening.

However, since there is a lot of talk about Gen Z and Gen Alpha to follow, and since I have referred to you as Gen X (or Boomers, or Millennials), I should give the topic some attention.

Firstly, we are working longer. While many people will still retire at sixty or sixty-five years old, many will continue to work, either because they have a financial need or because they aren't ready to stop.

Secondly, the change in generations is happening more frequently. We used to think of a new generation emerging every twenty years. Now it's more like every ten. This is because generations are formed by early experiences. Our values and perspectives on the world are shaped, in part, by events from our childhood. For the Millennials, 9/11 and the world events it triggered were a foundational memory, and now those foundations are influencing their decisions about how and where they work, how they raise their families and what matters to them.

These events are occurring more frequently because the world is changing more quickly. Therefore, the generations are getting narrower.[42]

This all means more generations will be working alongside each other. Potentially you will soon have Gen Alphas (born since 2010) in the workplace alongside young Boomers… that's five generations working with each other, with different early personality-forming experiences.

For Gen Z, the pandemic will have been one of those foundational events. Many Gen Zs had their education disrupted by Covid and many grew up in households that were financially affected by the pandemic. They have a 'short attention span' due to the amount of information they are exposed to (although, of course, they can dive into information they are interested in – they aren't goldfish).[43] Another way to think about this is that they make fast decisions about what to dive into and what to swipe on from, so you have to catch their attention if you want them to take any notice. They have been managing their brand online their whole lives, a skill that can be of huge value to an organisation. They only notice diversity when they don't see it. Just look around at your next in-person event. What would they see?

They are intolerant of intolerance and will call out unethical behaviour, even when that behaviour is demonstrated by someone significantly more senior. You may think that an 'all-hands meeting' is private and internal, but if you tell an off-colour joke expect it to be shared, for a meme made out of it or for it to become a sound, endlessly repeated, on TikTok.

Coming up behind them are the Gen Alphas, the true digital natives who have had access to a digital world since birth. Born since 2010, AI is natural to them. They expect to talk to their devices and have those devices talk back. They were children (if they were even born) of Covid and the long tail of its impact. If you think 'identity' is a complex minefield now, get ready. This is a generation who are diverse in the broadest sense and who may make lifestyle choices that previous generations find challenging, or at least confusing. They will expect their personal choices to be taken into account.

These are the people you are leaving your organisations to. They are starting their careers now and making choices about where they want to work or where they want to remain. They will be shocked by your clunky tech systems, by your random business-attire guidelines, by the lack of awareness around diversity, and by the stories you tell about what used to be acceptable workplace behaviour. When I talk about some of my BBC experiences, the Boomers and Gen Xers in the audience laugh in recognition. The Gen Zs stare back at me in horror.

Remember that, for the first time in living history, these are generations who are likely to feel less well-off than their parents. It will be hard for them to get on the property ladder or even rent a single occupancy home. Most likely, they will live with their parents or flat share for longer than previous generations.

Values are important to them. Well-being matters and they work to live rather than live to work (remember, these are massive generalisations). Eighty per cent of Gen Z employees want to work with a company whose values align with their own.[44] They are socially conscious, too. Greenwashing doesn't wash with them. You'll have to mean what you say and demonstrate your values in your actions, just as I have counselled in this book so far.

Gen Alpha are still children so we don't know how they will respond to work, but it's a pretty safe guess that they will have different expectations to workers born in the twentieth century.

If you want to attract and retain young talent, you'll need to look hard at how you lead and the environment you create for your people. There are increasing options either to work for companies that are ethical, less hierarchical and more inclusive, or to start a business for themselves. Barriers to entry have never been lower. There are probably cooler industries than yours and cooler brands, so, just from that perspective, there's a great deal of work to do. That is apart from the bigger imperative: for businesses to be a force for good in the world.

Business as a force for good in the world

The 2023 Edelman Trust Barometer[45] described Argentina, the USA, Spain, Sweden, South Africa and Colombia as 'severely polarised' – not only do people perceive the country as divided, but they believe those divisions cannot be overcome. Brazil, France, the UK, Japan, Italy, Mexico, South Korea, the Netherlands and Germany are in the 'in danger of severe polarisation' category.

The rich and powerful, hostile foreign governments, government leaders and journalists are all considered by the majority of people to be dividing forces, pulling people apart. As a breed, CEOs are not trusted and are seen as part of the problem, reinforcing the trend towards polarisation.

The 2024 report focuses on how technological innovation is perceived, and it's not good news for global trust. Thirty-nine per cent of people believe innovation is poorly managed and many believe society is changing too quickly and that they are being left behind. People expect business to take responsibility, not just for changes occurring in their own organisation, but changes occurring in society as a whole.[46]

At the same time, of the institutions represented in the survey, business is more trusted than governments, the media and NGOs. The public wants company CEOs to act on public policy issues such as climate change, discrimination, the wealth gap, immigration and innovation. Above all, people believe CEOs should take a stand on how employees are treated. A huge majority of people feel CEOs are obligated to pay fair wages, ensure their home community is safe and thriving, pay fair corporate taxes, ensure technology is used ethically and retrain employees when technological advances and changing specs of work require.

While people don't want business leaders to get involved in politics, they do expect companies to collaborate with governments, to hold themselves to high standards of ethics, to invest in their people and in local communities to restore economic optimism, and to advocate for the truth.

All of this points to a new expectation – that business can and should be a force for good in the world. Profits matter, of course – they keep the show on the road – but whether profits should be the number one, exclusive measure of success is another matter. There are increasing numbers of businesses which don't have financials as their primary metrics. Buurtzorg, a Dutch healthcare organisation, is run as a not-for-profit. It sets targets for billable hours of patient care, but, beyond that, there are few rules. Client satisfaction, quality of care, employee engagement and the number of self-managing teams are at least as important as profit.[47]

Patagonia[48] is another example of a business that prioritises its social responsibility, donating its profits to environmental causes and encouraging customers to repair and recycle their products rather than buying new ones.[49]

B Corps are only able to achieve certification if they can show that they balance profit with purpose and their impact on various stakeholders.

Of course, there are plenty of other companies who claim to have a broader mission than just making money, but what happens when there are tough decisions to make and a choice between a cheaper, more profitable option which requires sacrificing some of the other metrics such as employee well-being or environmental impact, versus a decision which will cost the company money but will uphold those other ESG-type metrics? Most companies are unwilling to uphold their 'values' if there is a financial price at stake. They create a hierarchy of importance, willing to sacrifice employee well-being or environmental targets in order to hit financial goals.

Even worse, in fact, is when the leadership of a company claims there is no 'hierarchy of importance' and that all priorities are equal, eg ESG and employee well-being *and* profit. These companies refuse to recognise (at least openly) that profit would have to be compromised in order to deliver on the other values. The result is that the board will make tough cost-cutting decisions to maintain profit margins but still expect their people, somehow, to hit all the other metrics, with fewer resources to do it. Jobs are cut to make cost-savings and report a higher EBIT, but the remaining employees are still expected to deliver high-quality products, meet timelines, hit environmental and social metrics and report in their engagement survey that they are loving the challenge. It is impossible, and, in trying to achieve these impossible expectations, people start to break.

By contrast, a company I am working with currently (and who therefore must remain anonymous) recently had to make some employees redundant because new technology meant they simply weren't needed. That company acquired a number of new businesses in order to provide work for anyone displaced by the new technology. The business says it cares about its people... and it demonstrated what it is willing to do to prove it.

As a world, we have become more cynical about authority figures and large institutions. For your business to thrive, to have the trust of its customers and generate trust among its employees, it will need to aim higher than hitting financial targets.

It's time to start asking difficult questions, highlighting tensions and initiating conversations, using the skills and approaches outlined in this book, about whether your company is one of the good guys or whether it is contributing to an unsustainable cocktail of short-termism, half-truths and inhumane expectations.

Business shapes our world

Our world looks the way it looks not because it was designed this way by politicians, but because it was designed this way by business. Everything from our education system, to when we eat, where we live, the clothes we wear, and the values that most of us live by are such because of the way we interact with businesses. If businesses were different, our world would be different.

In this case, it is not too far-fetched to say that considering all the ways your company could be a force for good in the world could truly revolutionise how we live. Do people find their lives meaningful, rewarding and enjoyable? Or do they find their lives tense, fearful, humdrum and empty? Is the world they inhabit optimistic? Do they feel they have agency over their lives? Are there opportunities? Do they feel their children have something to look forward to? Or do they feel pessimistic? Do they feel powerless? Do they feel glad that they won't be around to see what the future holds?

Every time you stand for business as a force for good, you play a part in making the world a better place. Or you can just keep your head down and let the status quo play out. It's up to you.

We never leave anyone behind

In my early days as a coach, I ran lots of training workshops. I was told that it was common practice to hand out 'happy sheets' at the end of these workshops to see if people liked the sessions. After everyone had gone home, we would sift through the happy sheets, carrying out a 'post-mortem' on what we had done and whether we would do something differently next time.

After a few of these, I wondered whether it was a helpful process. For one thing, the test of a workshop like this isn't whether people enjoyed the experience but whether they applied the tools and saw results. Someone can enjoy the workshop and do nothing with it. Someone else can find the workshop deeply uncomfortable but apply what they learnt and see a real impact.

In addition, we always went home disappointed. That one person who hated it would always stay in our mind and, no matter how many people loved it, the critique from that disgruntled individual would keep us awake at night. The only way we could feel better about ourselves was to say, 'Well, there's always one; you can't get it right for everyone.'

This attitude never sat right with me. Why couldn't we create a space where everyone could get value? It was too easy to say that the person who didn't appreciate our work was the one with the problem. What if we rejected the notion that 'there's always one' and set out instead never to leave anyone behind?

When I talk about some of the insights in this book with leaders, family or friends, I often hear, 'But not everyone can work this way.' In other words, 'Some people might be able to take ownership, connect with their emotions, come up with ideas, work in collaboration, think for themselves or take initiative. But a lot of people can't or don't want to. What do you do about them?'

As you look around your business, you might feel the same. There are the people who are up for a challenge, for learning and for being outside of their comfort zone – and then there's everyone else. In Blaire's idealised version of the world, what do we do about these folk?

My first response is to ask, 'How would we know what people are capable of? We have never created a world where people get to find out.'

Our education system guarantees that a percentage of children *must* fail. Grade boundaries are adjusted every year to ensure only a small percentage get the highest grades. No matter how hard you work or how well you do, the percentage of children failing is pre-determined.

In addition, our education system isn't designed for the world we have today, let alone the world of tomorrow.

We are still testing for the ability to memorise facts. We only measure what is easy to measure (just like we have done in business). The education system focuses on what it can test for, ideally with answers that don't leave much room for subjective judgement so that results are 'fair'. Those children who do well have often learnt to game the system, understanding what will be given a mark and what won't. They don't bother learning anything that doesn't get a mark and they certainly don't waste valuable exam time adding ideas, opinions and any further research they have done when they know it won't enhance their grade.

Schools are very much hierarchies, with children still calling their teacher Miss, Mr, Mrs or even Sir. When you need more discipline, you are sent to the head teacher's office. No surprise that, years later at work, being called to a meeting with 'The Big Boss' makes you wonder what you've done wrong.

Many leaders I've worked with over the years are frustrated by how unprepared new recruits are for the world of work. They may have technical knowledge, but they often lack awareness of how to contribute to the organisation, how to take ownership of finding answers, how to ask the right questions and how to speak to those they perceive as authority figures. They are still operating by the rules of school.

More than that, many of the qualities we need now and in future in our human employees simply don't get recognised or developed at school. Creative problem-solving, emotional intelligence, taking the initiative, listening, being curious, challenging norms and conventions, expressing opinions and embracing conflicts of perspective, connecting with your own deeper sense of purpose or helping others articulate theirs, enjoying difference and diversity, being aware of global trends, distinguishing between fact and opinion, marketing and truth, strategies to keep healthy in mind and body, how to budget and find a good deal, how the tax system works, who has the power in our world and how they use that power, who has the money in our world and how they use that money, how to think for yourself, how to be a valuable member of society, how to plan for a working life that may go into your seventies and a life that might last eight or nine decades or more...

So, when we brush aside huge swathes of people saying, 'They won't be able to function in a world that requires them to think and are only suited to following orders', and even, 'They don't *want* to think, they just want to do what they are told', we are ignoring generations of programming. We do not live in a meritocracy, and many people grow up believing their adult lives are inevitably going to be humdrum, that their work cannot be meaningful and that, at best, they will earn enough money to give their families more than they had growing up. In truth, as Kay Sargent said in my interview with her,[50] many young people are going to be less well-off than their parents even though we are working harder than ever before.

My second reaction to the question 'What about the people who can't do this kind of work, or don't want to?' is this: I do not underestimate the enjoyment and meaning that comes from different kinds of work. Getting your hands dirty, organising things and people, becoming a masterful craftsperson, becoming an expert at a repetitive task, work that doesn't require much thought... there is value in this work for humans too. Sometimes it feels good to clear out the stockroom. Sometimes it's pleasurable to have an afternoon doing mindless paperwork. Some people will want work which doesn't require them to be intellectually focused, either because of the way their brain works or because that's not what they are looking for from their job. We want people of different abilities to be able to find work and contribute in ways that work for them.

If we are to approach the future of work from a humane perspective, we need to create jobs that appeal to different personality types, different neuro-types, different physical types, different wants and desires, and even different moods. At times, I have been frustrated with my work, feeling that the expectations of my family forced me down an intellectual path which resulted in my body being simply a machine for carrying my brain around.

To combat this, I have learnt to grow vegetables in the garden, I've taken up working out with weights at the gym and, from time to time, I will teach myself a skill like knitting or crochet as a way to connect with my body and its value, not just my brain. When I bring a home-grown courgette into the house, I know that it is probably the most expensive courgette in the world, requiring unfathomable hours by me in the garden plus a few tonnes of compost and a shed-full of hand tools to produce. I could pick one up from the supermarket, but there's something rewarding about kneeling on the earth, getting muck under my fingernails and finding a fully grown courgette under a jungle of massive leaves which adds to my sense of meaning and purpose. I don't have to grow it myself. I want to.

Just because we could get a machine to do a job, doesn't mean we should. Sometimes, we will want to reserve certain types of work for humans even if we could mechanise them, because we don't want a world where people are left behind. Just because we can mass-produce something, doesn't mean we shouldn't value the craft that humans bring to creating that same object by hand. Just because AI could write a box-office smash movie, doesn't mean we should replace all the writers. Right now, we are seeing this particular threat play out with the SAG-AFTRA strike, and we will see more industrial action along these lines in future as humans work out where AI can be a liberator of human talent and ingenuity and where it poses a genuine threat to our world.

Let's not be blasé about this technology, and let's use it to create a world which is better for humans. Let's not leave anyone behind.

Taking the long view

Humans are always balancing short-term benefits with long-term benefits. The two are often mutually exclusive. I can eat all the cake today and feel good in the moment. Or I can prioritise my long-term health by not eating all the cake and feeling good in the future. Humans are operating with two brains (I am simplifying, of course). We have our ancient brain, which is about the here and now. The food is there, I am hungry, I eat the food. Any long-term planning, such as storing nuts for winter, is instinctive rather than thoughtful.

Pasted on top of that ancient brain is our more recently evolved brain. This brain can reason, plan and imagine, and these two brains are in constant conflict. Hence, I both want the cake now *and* I want long-term health. Which brain will win?

Businesses are run by humans, so they also have two brains. There is the brain that wants the short-term return – hitting this quarter's EBITDA, getting a pat on the back from group HQ for being on budget and on time, and seeing the share price rise at the announcement of some initiative. Then there's the brain that wants to create an environment where employees thrive, that wants the business to contribute to the betterment of the community in which it is located and that wants to future-proof itself by thinking creatively about how to adapt to changing technology and be a force for good in the world.

Typically, the short-term and long-term business benefits are mutually exclusive, too, and, a bit like most people in the face of a delicious piece of cake, the short-term wins. The system of reporting and accounting, people's career ambitions, the pace of change and a barrage of unpredictable emergencies (like Covid-19) make it easier to take a short-term perspective.

We all know about business leaders who pretty-up their organisations to make them look good ahead of a sale, and it's only once the new owners take a look under the metaphorical bonnet that they see the short-term wins had a long-term price which they will now have to pay. We all know of business leaders who launch an initiative to great applause and then quickly use that success to get a big new job somewhere else before the mess hits the fan and the fundamental flaws in the programme come to the surface. We all know business leaders who cut costs to the bone to boost profits for newspaper headlines (and for their own reputations), while those working in the business can see the price they will be paying further down the road.

There is a principle gaining traction called 'The 7th Generation Principle.'[51] This philosophy is based on an ancient Iroquois idea that, 'In our every deliberation, we must consider the impact of our decisions on the next seven generations.' (You can hear me discuss this concept with Miranda Willems in this chapter's interview.) When we step back from short-termism and consider how our decisions might be perceived by generations past and how they will impact generations in future, we are forced to step away from our self-interests and consider instead what makes a decision sustainable for the future.

One way to think about this is to picture you, the current generation, at the centre, with three generations of ancestors behind you and three future generations ahead. In this way, you are communing with your great-grandparents and with your great-grandchildren. Any further back or forward and it is hard to really connect, but, with luck, you knew at least one of your grandparents, so your great-grandparents are within reach. Or perhaps you know their names, where they lived, and maybe you've seen photos. Equally, if you have children or are close to a child (niece, nephew, friend's child), you can maybe imagine them as a grandparent. Maybe you can imagine their grandchildren, sitting at their feet while they hear about growing up in the early twenty-first century.

My own grandma lived to the age of ninety-nine. She was a real character who put her longevity down to a glass of Scotch every night and to seeing each stage in her life as the best stage. Occasionally, when I've been struggling in my own life, after a breakup or when I've been worried about my business, for instance, I've called my grandma to mind and asked, 'If I had ninety-nine years of perspective on this problem, how would I react to it?' Invariably, I realise that I wouldn't worry too much about it. Life has ups and downs, moments of drama and moments of fear, but normally we get through them, learn from them and barely remember the details after a while. This has helped me so many times.

The 7th Generation Principle allows us to tap into this kind of perspective, to recognise that our short-term desires, pressures, conflicts and emergencies are probably not as serious as they seem. If our great-grandparents were watching, what insights would they have? How would they judge how we are responding? If they were in the room with us, what questions would they have? What concerns? What context could they offer? Would they be proud of how we are handling the situation? Could we explain what we were doing and why? Would we feel comfortable doing that, or somehow ashamed? When I talk to audiences about trust, I sometimes say that a good test of whether you should do something or not is how you would feel if your mum found out. Would you rather she didn't know? If so, maybe you shouldn't be doing it.

Bringing the 'ancestors' into the room is a way to connect with your higher self and ask bigger questions than the ones you're asking when you are deep inside a problem or situation. Perhaps, you want your boss to like you or you want to avoid conflict, but, if your ancestors were in the room, would you feel obliged to speak from the heart and tell your truth, rather than take the easy option of avoiding a disagreement? Would you feel obliged to be your best self if you were being observed by past generations?

What about future generations? If your great-grandchildren were in the room, their little faces looking up at you, and you saw in their eyes the world you've left for them, how would you feel about the short-term decisions you're making today? Could you, with a clear conscience, justify what you're doing?

Wales is the only country to have a Well-being of the Future Generations Act (although the concept is gaining traction in other parts of the world such as the Netherlands). The country's Future Generations Commissioner is tasked with protecting and promoting the needs of future generations,[52] considering issues like some of those discussed in this book – the implications of AI and bot technology on jobs and what that might mean for our children and grand-children, what a longer life expectancy might mean for our health and the healthcare sector, and how to plan long term to address problems such as poverty, inequality and climate change.

The Well-being of Future Generations Act sets an expectation that public bodies in Wales work towards a single purpose, with seven well-being goals to work towards. It is clearly stated that these public bodies must work to achieve all seven, not just one or two.

What if your organisation had a 'future genera-tions leader', team, co-operative or community? What if decisions had to be considered through a seven-generation lens? What if you 'invited' ancestors and future generations to the conversation either by imagining their presence or even by literally involv-ing other generations in your business, to share their perspectives and help you think differently about the right and just thing to do in any situation?

If technology could liberate people to do funda-mentally human work, thinking from the perspective of future and past generations would be one way we would spend our time. Perhaps we would find ways to unshackle ourselves from the magnetic draw of short-termism which determines so many decisions, and take more responsibility for the long-term impact of our decisions.

When a person is standing in front of a piece of cake deciding whether to eat it, sometimes the long-term perspective wins. Typically, that is because that individual is able to bring their future self into the present. They have a powerful connection with who they will be tomorrow, next year or next decade. They know at that moment how their future self will hope they acted.

Bringing that same perspective into our businesses could have the same impact. We would see, in the moment, how a short-term decision to cancel the company summer barbeque would save a few thousand dollars but send a powerful message to our people that we don't mean it when we say they are our most important asset. It's not worth the true price – the broken trust with our people.

This is where I am challenging you to stand, right in the centre of the three previous generations and the three generations to come, and secure the future of your business as a force for good in the world.

Action 6: Speak up and be a critical friend

To take risks, to iterate ideas, to be agile and open to constant change and disruption we need to have real skin in the game. We need to feel not only empowered or autonomous but also part of something bigger, where we make a difference and where our actions have consequences.

A leader needs to be brave. They need to break rules which have kept them safe throughout their career and which could be uncomfortable for both them and others.

They need to speak up.

We've all been in meetings where we've not liked the way a conversation is going, where we can see that the stated values of the organisation are about to be compromised and where our people are going to be the ones to pay the price, and just before we say something, a voice in our head says 'No':

- Don't put a spanner in the works at this stage. If you were going to say something you should have said it earlier.

- Everyone else seems OK with it, who are you to object?

- Maybe you can't have it all – maybe you have to prioritise pleasing the market and showing continual quarterly growth, and sacrifices have to be made.

- It's nearly lunch break. No one is going to thank you for bringing this up now!

- I'm going to let this one go and save my disruption for something else that I feel more confident about (and where less is at stake for me).

There are unspoken rules in most organisations about how and when (and to whom) you are allowed to speak up. You can speak up:

- When you've been asked for your opinion
  (as long as you've been promised that bold and
  unpopular ideas are welcome)

- If you have a constructive alternative suggestion

- With authority figures, but the timing has to
  be right

- With some people but not others, because of their
  personality, and only if you use certain language
  and influencing skills so that you don't upset or
  offend or make them feel threatened or 'wrong'

- But not about systemic issues which are too big
  to fix (like the Victorian beliefs which underpin
  attitudes, or dismantling the reporting structure,
  or putting an end to the need to show a growth
  in EBITDA every quarter)

- But don't get a reputation for being negative
  and critical

- But without sharing certain information which
  might freak junior people out

This means that, in our current system, suggestions
and feedback are always within a range of acceptabil-
ity and don't threaten the status quo.

For business to truly become a force for good and
transform in the ways necessary to be fit for the future,
you'll need to speak up about big, hairy, uncomfortable issues. You'll have to tear the status quo down.
You'll have to shine a light on norms and conventions
that others have thought were best left in the shadows.

213

A caveat – don't misunderstand me. I'm not suggesting you throw your weight around, mouthing off about every gripe you have to whoever is standing nearby, never taking responsibility for the impact you have on others or for doing something about what you're so unhappy about. A workplace should be a civilised place where people have respect for others and for the impact they have on others. Especially in a humane workplace where human beings are truly valued, we need to use our emotional intelligence. After all, it's that which differentiates us from the nonhuman, AI workforce. Being just as willing to listen (see Chapter 5) as to speak up matters if you want to access the wisdom of every single human in the organisation in service of the organisation's purpose. You can't access that wisdom when you're taking up all the airspace in every room you are in.

However, why are you in the room if you aren't going to contribute? It would be better not to show up at the meeting if your only contribution is to think something and not say it. You may as well be doing something else, like organising your emails or watching TikToks on your phone.

Your value comes from your unique contribution to the richness of the picture. You've been hired for your perspective. That perspective will come from your values, your experiences, your biases, your creativity, and your willingness to question and to be wrong.

To create an adult-adult environment where people break free from the Industrial-Age hardwiring of doffing their cap to the most senior person in the room or conforming to age-old conventions which led to a compliant and machine-like workforce, you have to start speaking up, clearly and concisely.

You have to bite the bullet and begin. This starts with inner reflection, and then speaking up:

- Who do I need to talk to and what do I want to tell them?

- Are my intentions pure? Are they for the well-being of the business, service to the client or for the benefit of the people in the organisation?

- Am I speaking from my values or my ego?

- Am I lashing out, trying to score points or trying to hide my failings?

- Am I speaking from a place of 100% support for the success of the business, the clients and the people within the organisation?

We call this approach the '*critical friend*'.

The 'critical friend' combines the best of being a friend (100% belief and support) with having a critical eye. By this, I don't mean 'finding fault'. I mean 'critique-al', a willingness to critique. This might include:

- Challenging others to think bigger

- Challenging others to be practical

- Giving feedback

- Pointing out where their energy seems to be focused

- Calling out habits that aren't serving the business

- Questioning the assumptions others may be making

- Sharing experiences

- Sharing opinions

- Offering alternative suggestions

- Playing what others have said back to them

- Stopping discussions going around in circles

- Noticing what the group keeps skipping over

- Noticing the stories the group is telling itself

- Noticing where the group is stuck

- Pointing the group towards other experts or sources of advice

The leaders we need today are willing to do this for others and for the business.

When combined with the other actions already described in previous chapters – listening so hard you might change your mind, questioning conventional wisdom, creating a humane environment, extending your willingness to trust, giving away your power – this willingness to speak up and speak out about matters of principle binds you to others, creating a community in which important conversations about the future can happen.

When you openly, honestly, in good faith, with vulnerability and humility, put 'purpose' and 'being a force for good' on the table, you can start a reformation in your business, and in the world.

LISTEN NOW

Miranda Willems is a social innovator for Future Generations.[53] She works with companies and other groups to help them perceive from a seven-generation perspective.

In this thought-provoking conversation, she describes what it means to sit between generations to come and our great ancestors. It's so important that we listen to the voices of younger colleagues and those with different perspectives, especially those who provoke us to see the world through different lenses. I learnt a lot. I hope you will as well.

You can listen to the interview at **www. buzzsprout.com/2250059/13678763**, or listen to any of the other interviews here: **https:// punksinsuitshowtoleadtheworkplacereformation. buzzsprout.com**

Summary

There is an urgency to this call for change in how we run businesses, their ethos, their values and the way they use both human and nonhuman potential. Business has the potential to be a force for good in the world by committing to missions that go beyond short-term profits and quick wins for shareholders. Business leaders must acknowledge that doing the right thing for society, for employees and for customers sometimes has a financial cost, and then they need to do the right thing anyway.

As you stand on the cusp of this revolution, you have the opportunity to bring the full diversity of people along with you, creating opportunities for them to discover their talents, tastes, preferences and purpose, and use those for the benefit of the business and those it serves.

Business shapes our world. Therefore, if you are unhappy with the way that world is, it's to business you should look for solutions, not to politicians. Rather than taking the short-term view, stand between your ancestors and your great-grandchildren and take the perspective of seven generations.

From there, you can become a critical friend – 100% believing in the potential of the business and the people within it to be a force for good, and committed to asking tough questions, speaking your truth and being vigilant in safeguarding the higher purpose of the enterprise.

Questions to consider

- In what ways is our business *not* a force for good in the world?

- What does, or could, our business stand for?

- If we meant it, what price would we be willing to pay to be true to that mission and ethos?

- Where do we compromise, in big and small ways, on the things that we say matter to us?

- If we weren't to 'leave anyone behind', what would we do?

- How could we create space for people to do work that is meaningful and purposeful for them, embracing the diversity of their wants and needs?

- How do I connect better with the 'ancestors'?

- How do I connect better with my future grandchildren?

- If I listened to these generations, what questions would I ask? What observations would I make? What would matter and what would not?

- Where do I hold back from speaking up? How do I justify that?

- If I were a true critical friend to the business and to my colleagues, what would I do differently?

CHAPTER 7

PUNKS in SUITS

Punks In Suits
Conclusion

I 've always enjoyed a good superhero movie. *Superman* (the Christopher Reeve version) gave me my first grown-up career ambition. I was taken by feisty Lois Lane and decided that I would be her when I grew up.

Some years ago, I decided to set myself the challenge of watching thirty superhero movies in thirty days. Other keynote conference speakers set themselves challenges to climb treacherous mountains or break world records, but I was looking for something I could do sitting down.

I thought that I could use the insights from the superhero movies to add flavour to my speeches, maybe by talking about how leaders could become superheroes in their organisations. Something like that. It turned out that I had the opposite realisation.

In the movies, we typically take a mild-mannered, invisible person and turn them, with the donning of a special outfit, into a hero or heroine. They are, if you like, your conventional leader. They hide behind the mask and the muscle suit, presenting themselves as 'beyond human', with special powers that leave ordinary mortals in the dust.

But I have described in this book a type of leadership which is fundamentally human. All those weird corners of your personality, the unique qualities which make you 'you', your capacity for strong, complex, conflicting emotions, your inevitable mistakes and missteps, the imposter syndrome and the inner voices that tell you you're about to be found out, the person who runs a really important online meeting about the future of your division and then pops downstairs to empty the washing machine... that's what today's and tomorrow's leadership needs.

To be an effective leader now means taking off the mask, unpeeling the muscle suit and revealing who you are to others and to yourself. To grow as a leader, you need to grow as a person. That might require therapy, coaching, reading self-help books, listening to podcasts which inspire you, taking on new challenges that are outside your comfort zone, meditating, learning from people you find difficult to hear, and doing that for the rest of your working life.

This new form of leadership isn't about being better than others. It's about being committed to your own growth and creating space for others to grow. You aren't superhuman. You are just someone who is curious, open-minded, willing to walk towards what is uncomfortable and then change in the light of what you learn.

If you do that, you'll be capable of accepting this call to adventure.

The call to adventure

Here is what I'm challenging you to do:

1. **Embrace the humanity of people rather than treating them like machines.** We have ever-more sophisticated machines, which means we can find ways to liberate people from the kinds of work that machines can do better and find work that is innately human for them to do instead. There is room for everyone to bring their humanity to their work, whether that is their capacity to be a cheerful presence for others, to do beautiful work with their hands, to think, discuss and debate, to lead others, to coach others, to connect with customers and clients... The technology is evolving incredibly fast. Leaders have got to think about what this means for their human colleagues and work out what humans can offer that is unique.

2. **Create trusting environments.** We've created organisations in which people constantly compete for attention, recognition, resources, power, influence, promotions and favour. This leads

to distrust between people. How can we work together in collaboration, develop great solutions and find work meaningful and rewarding in that context? To change work, we need to focus on creating trusting environments so everyone feels safe bringing their whole self to what they do.

3. **Deconstruct hierarchical thinking.** The hierarchy keeps information locked in disparate parts of the organisation and is used as currency in internal power struggles. If the only reward you get for your sacrifice is a reward to your ego, you'll take it. If nothing more meaningful is on offer, you'll cling to the badges of power that you've accumulated. If we can dismantle this hierarchical thinking, however, share information, push decision-making out to the people in the best place to make decisions, then we can offer something more meaningful than an ego boost. We can offer truly meaningful work and people will feel they are really making a difference.

4. **Think differently about what a leader does.** This kind of leadership is about clearing a path for others to be great. It's about looking for tensions, removing barriers, waving the beacon from the horizon to remind people about the bigger purpose, and then ensuring there is as little in the way as possible. It's not necessarily high profile. It doesn't necessarily feed the ego, but without leadership of this kind, people can't work in

collaboration and find sustainable solutions. Leadership is about being the enabler of others.

5. **Always be changing.** Change is a constant. It's a cliché but it's true. You need to be willing to change if things are to change. You need to understand the journey of change, and the role that emotion plays in the success of an organisation as it constantly adapts and flexes. The more emotionally sophisticated you are and the more open you are to taking people along on the journey for real, the better the organisation will get and the more meaningful the work will become.

6. **Focus on business as a force for good.** How businesses treat their employees, the impact they have on the wider community in which they operate, their customers, their stakeholders, their suppliers and partners, the health of the planet, the role they take influencing public policy, the investments they make in good causes (or not), the messages they send out in their advertising and marketing about what has value and what is important (or what doesn't have value and isn't important) becomes reality to a far greater degree than anything a politician does. To be a force for good in the world, a business requires leaders like you to consider its impact on the world around it, and how it can do more good than harm.

If you do all this, here is what will happen:

1. **People will enjoy their work.** Work can and should be meaningful. It takes up so much of our lives that it would be tragic if it wasn't. People don't have to be literally changing the world for this to be true. Creating something with their hands, being a listening ear for others, making a customer's day, being appreciated, learning something, helping someone, or using the money they earned to make their home a safe and welcoming place... there are myriad ways work can be meaningful. This is reason enough to address the issues with how we currently do things and the experience people have of working for our organisations. Life is precious. To spend years of it in an environment which causes relentless stress, or which is simply unsatisfying, feels like a waste. You can do something about this.

2. **Humanity will be valued.** People have so much to offer that is currently untapped. Being too busy to think, to really connect with ourselves and with others, even to answer emails in a timely and thoughtful way, forces our humanity to one side. We are just trying to get everything done. If we could put humanity at the heart of our work and find ways for tech to do the rest, we could bring far more of what we have to offer to what we do. We could think, we could care, we could help each other. If we wanted to spend a few hours doing mundane work because

we wanted a break from thinking, we would! A humane environment would allow for different kinds of work for different kinds of people and at different times, but work would be humane and, as a result, our world would be more humane.

3. **Work will be fairer.** Exclusion is built into our current system. Try as we might to embrace inclusion, we are fighting the DNA of our organisations. As long as you have internal competition for resources, recognition, power, access to information and decision-making rights, you will have exclusion. You will have winners and losers. Winners have a vested interest in maintaining a system that works for them, which means excluding others. But when leaders are willing to give away power, to be curious, to go towards tensions and engage different voices in understanding and addressing those tensions, when leaders are committed to dismantling centres of power, then you have a chance of creating a fair workplace where challenges to the status quo are welcomed.

4. **Sustainability will be the new success criteria.** A short-term win today usually has a long-term cost tomorrow. By switching the emphasis away from short-term wins, we can start thinking about what makes sense in the long term. Most people do care about the world they are leaving for future generations, but it's been hard to prioritise that because people have been rewarded

for short-term solutions. The approach I've described, of standing on the horizon waving the beacon to remind people where you are going, means that a sense of mission and purpose drives decision-making. There isn't a prize for short-term wins that take you further from the destination or make the road ahead more difficult. The prize is only for solutions that address tensions and clear a path that takes you closer to the bigger, more meaningful mission – a mission your future grandchildren will thank you for.

Where do you start?

In every chapter, I've outlined an action that will get you started. I hope you will model new approaches every day and that other people will notice. I hope that you will talk about what you are doing, about what you are learning, and give people the opportunity to try it too.

Together, you will come up with ideas to address those meaty issues in your business. It's not for me to tell you what structure will work in your organisation, or what your business mission should be. I am not going to prescribe a solution to problems like the endless, time-wasting meetings, nor will I design a DE&I initiative for you. That's your job. You and the people in your organisation are capable of coming up with all the solutions for your business.

But you have to see those tensions first. Then you need to peel away all the Victorian-Age hardwiring that prevents you from having the conversations and thinking of the ideas that will address those tensions.

In this way, you won't just have a solution to today's pressing issues. You will have baked into the DNA of your organisation the capacity to think for yourselves and make change yourselves.

There is something radical about this idea. For too long, 'change' was seen as something temporary. The status quo, the steady state, was what we aimed for. Only when the tensions were so painful that they could no longer be ignored did we say, 'OK, we have to change this.' Then we would propose sweeping changes, to the whole organisation, all at once, in the hope that, once it was done, we could return to a steady state.

We know that isn't the reality now, if it ever was.

Change must be an everyday occurrence. We need to be constantly iterating and tinkering. That's why the people in the organisation need those skills. Change can't be outsourced.

Start wherever you want. What are you most resistant to trying? Start there. That's where the most learning is for you.

Punks in suits

What I loved most about my month watching super-hero films was the quotable quotes.

'With great power comes great responsibility.'

— *Spider-Man*[54]

'Heroes are made by the path they choose, not the powers they are graced with.'

— *Iron Man*[55]

'The fate of your planet rests not in the hands of gods. It rests in the hands of mortals.'

— *Thor*[56]

One of my favourites is from the film *Kick-Ass 2*.[57] The quote gave me the title for this book and my keynote address: 'There's no room for punks in suits. Just real heroes who can really kick ass.'

The problem with this quote, though, is that it is back-to-front in the real world.

There are two kinds of punks. There's the American way of using the term to mean a worthless or rude young person – someone who thinks they are tough but it's all for show. They might hide behind aggressive language and behaviour, tough-looking clothes and a gang of other 'tough guys', but inside they are afraid, lacking self-awareness or any tools beyond aggression to make their lives better.

And then there are the punks of the 70s (and since). We tend to think about the music and the hairstyles, but punk was and is more than that. Punks embrace uniqueness and expressing who they are. They reject conformity, the establishment and conventional ideas about what is acceptable and 'normal', questioning old beliefs in an effort to be authentic and free.

In other words, they embody many of the qualities I've described in this book.

The old style of leadership was about heroes kicking ass, wielding their power and trying to get others to conform. It was about being a superhuman who is simply better than others and therefore deserving of the authority that came with increasingly grand job titles, decision-making rights and access to sensitive information.

You don't need a Mohican or safety pins all over your clothes to adopt something of the punk mindset. You can still wear a suit if you like. You can still have a full-time job, a nice home, value good manners and treat people with kindness. At the same time, underneath, you can be continually looking for the flaws in the system, the ways that we live and work that prevent you from expressing your true, authentic self, and get in the way of others doing the same.

If I were to re-write the *Kick-Ass* quote as a philosophy for leadership, then, I would put it this way:

'There's no room for heroes kicking ass. Just real people willing to reveal a bit of the punk underneath their suit.'

References

1   For more information on Kay Sargent, see www.hok.com, accessed 3 January 2024
2   World Economic Forum, 'Future of Jobs Report 2023' (30 April 2023), www.weforum.org/reports/the-future-of-jobs-report-2023/digest, accessed 3 January 2024
3   Ibid.
4   Ibid.
5   Ibid.
6   Ibid.
7   Nilekani, N, 'A New Foundation for Trust in Technology', Edelman (2022), www.edelman.com/trust/edelman-trust-institute/publication-2022/new-foundation-trust-technology, accessed 3 January 2024
8   Gallagher, J, 'New superbug-killing antibiotic discovered using AI', *BBC* (25 May 2023), www.bbc.co.uk/news/health-65709834, accessed 3 January 2024
9   World Economic Forum, 'Future of Jobs Report 2023' (30 April 2023), www.weforum.org/reports/the-future-of-jobs-report-2023/digest, accessed 3 January 2024
10 Ibid.
11 Ibid.

12   Price, D, 'On the Insidious "Laziness Lie" at the Heart of the American Myth', *Literary Hub* (6 January 2021), https://lithub.com/on-the-insidious-laziness-lie-at-the-heart-of-the-american-myth, accessed 3 January 2024

13   Marquet, LD, *Leadership Is Language* (Penguin Random House, 2020)

14   'Average Working Hours (Statistical Data 2023)', Clockify (no date), https://clockify.me/working-hours, accessed 3 January 2024

15   Lucas, S, 'Even Medieval Peasants Got More Vacation Than You', *Inc.* (7 November 2016), www.inc.com/suzanne-lucas/even-medieval-peasants-got-more-vacation-time-than-you-do.html, accessed 3 January 2024

16   Hewlett, SA and Luce, CB, 'Extreme Jobs: The dangerous allure of the 70-hour workweek', *Harvard Business Review* (December 2008), https://hbr.org/2006/12/extreme-jobs-the-dangerous-allure-of-the-70-hour-workweek, accessed 3 January 2024

17   Edelman, '2023 Edelman Trust Barometer: Global Report' (January 2023), www.edelman.com/trust/2023/trust-barometer, accessed 3 January 2024

18   Edelman, '20 years of trust' (2023), www.edelman.com/20yearsoftrust, accessed 3 January 2024

19   Edelman, '2023 Edelman Trust Barometer: Global Report' (January 2023), www.edelman.com/trust/2023/trust-barometer, accessed 3 January 2024

20   Achor, S, Reece, A, Rosen Kellerman, G and Robichaux, A, '9 Out of 10 People Are Willing to Earn Less Money to Do More Meaningful Work', *Harvard Business Review* (6 November 2018), https://hbr.org/2018/11/9-out-of-10-people-are-willing-to-earn-less-money-to-do-more-meaningful-work, accessed 3 January 2024

21   Dhue, S and Epperson, S, 'Most Workers Want Their Employer to Share Their Values – 56% won't even consider a workplace that doesn't, survey finds', *CNBC* (1 July 2022), www.cnbc.com/2022/07/01/most-workers-want-their-employer-to-share-their-values.html, accessed 3 January 2024

22   Office of National Statistics, 'Is Hybrid Working Here To Stay?' (23 May 2022), www.ons.gov.uk/employmentandlabourmarket/peopleinwork/employmentandemployeetypes/articles/ishybridworkingheretostay/2022-05-23, accessed 3 January 2024

23 Achor, S, Reece, A, Rosen Kellerman, G and Robichaux, A, '9 Out of 10 People Are Willing to Earn Less Money to Do More Meaningful Work', *Harvard Business Review* (6 November 2018), https://hbr.org/2018/11/9-out-of-10-people-are-willing-to-earn-less-money-to-do-more-meaningful-work, accessed 3 January 2024

24 Bromley, T, Lauricella, T and Shaninger, B, 'Making Work Meaningful From the C-suite to the Frontline', McKinsey (28 June 2021), www.mckinsey.com/capabilities/people-and-organizational-performance/our-insights/the-organization-blog/making-work-meaningful-from-the-c-suite-to-the-frontline, accessed 3 January 2024

25 Ross, MC, '7 Surprising Benefits of Doing Meaningful Work', Marie-Claire Ross (8 February 2023), www.marie-claireross.com/blog/9-benefits-of-meaningful-work, accessed 3 January 2024

26 Lencioni, P, 'Teamwork: The Five Dysfunctions of a Team', Table Group (no date), www.tablegroup.com/topics-and-resources/teamwork-5-dysfunctions, accessed 3 January 2024

27 Edelman, '2023 Edelman Trust Barometer: Global Report' (January 2023), www.edelman.com/trust/2023/trust-barometer, accessed 3 January 2024

28 Palmer, B, *What's Wrong with Work?* (Wiley, 2010)

29 Semler, R, 'Ricardo Semler: Radical wisdom for a company, a school, a life' (2015) https://youtu.be/k4vzhweOefs, accessed 3 January 2024

30 Laloux, F, *Reinventing Organisations* (Nelson Parker, 2014)

31 May, C and Sturgess-Durden, A, *Made Without Managers* (Right Book Company, 2023)

32 Stinson, L, 'The First Org Chart Ever Made Is a Masterpiece of Data Design', *Wired* (18 March 2014), www.wired.com/2014/03/stunningly-complex-organization-chart-19th-century, accessed 3 January 2024

33 'The Evolution of Org Charts: From the 1850s to now', Organimi (13 July 2020) www.organimi.com/the-evolution-of-org-charts, accessed 3 January 2024

34 Kegan, R, Lahey, L, Fleming, A and Miller, M, 'Making Business Personal', *Harvard Business Review* (April 2014), https://hbr.org/2014/04/making-business-personal, accessed 3 January 2024

35 Marquet, LD, *Leadership Is Language* (Penguin Random House, 2020)

36 Kegan, R, Lahey, L, Fleming, A and Miller, M, 'Making Business Personal', *Harvard Business Review* (April 2014), https://hbr.org/2014/04/making-business-personal, accessed 3 January 2024

37 Edelman, 'Only One-Third of Consumers Trust Most of the Brands They Buy', Edelman (18 June 2019), www.edelman.com/news-awards/only-one-third-of-consumers-trust-most-of-the-brands-they-buy, accessed 3 January 2024

38 Chambers, S, 'Customer Perception and How to Manage It Effectively', HelpScout (23 January 2023), www.helpscout.com/blog/customer-perception, accessed 3 January 2024

39 Katzenbach, JR and Smith, DK, 'The Discipline of Teams', *Harvard Business Review* (March–April 1993), https://hbr.org/1993/03/the-discipline-of-teams-2, accessed 3 January 2024

40 Katie, B, *Loving What Is* (Harmony Books, 2002)

41 Marquet, LD, *Leadership Is Language* (Penguin Random House, 2020)

42 Iberdrola, 'Generation Alpha Will Lead a 100% Digital World' (2023), www.iberdrola.com/talent/alpha-generation, accessed 3 January 2024

43 McKinsey & Company, *Mind the Gap* (29 November 2022), www.mckinsey.com/~/media/mckinsey/email/genz/2022/11/29/2022-11-29b.html, accessed 3 January 2024

44 Galarza, A, 'How to Engage Generation-Z in the Workplace', *Forbes* (15 February 2023), www.forbes.com/sites/forbeshumanresourcescouncil/2023/02/15/how-to-engage-generation-z-in-the-workplace, accessed 3 January 2024

45 Edelman, '2023 Edelman Trust Barometer: Global Report' (January 2023), www.edelman.com/trust/2023/trust-barometer, accessed 3 January 2024

46 Edelman, '2024 Edelman Trust Barometer: Global Report' (January 2024), www.edelman.com/trust/2024/trust-barometer, accessed 9 January 2024

47 Sandino, T and Bernstein, E, Lobb, A, 'This Company Lets Employees Take Charge – Even with Life and Death Decisions', Harvard Business School (23 June 2023), https://hbswk.hbs.edu/item/this-company-lets-employees-take-charge-buurtzorg, accessed 6 December 2023

48 www.patagonia.com/returns.html, accessed 3 January 2024

49 May, M, 'Patagonia Founder Gives Away All
Company Profits to Fight Climate Crisis', Fundraising.
co.uk, (15 September 2022), https://fundraising.
co.uk/2022/09/15/patagonia-founder-gives-away-
all-company-profits-to-fight-climate-crisis, accessed
3 January 2024

50 If you've not already done so, listen to it here: www.
buzzsprout.com/2250059/13618085

51 '7th Generation Principle', Seven Generations International
Foundation Australia (no date), http://7genfoundation.
org/7th-generation, accessed 3 January 2024

52 'Future Generations Commissioner for Wales', Future
Generations (no date), www.futuregenerations.wales/
about-us/future-generations-commissioner, accessed 3
January 2024

53 For more information about Miranda, see www.linkedin.
com/in/mirandawillems, accessed 3 January 2024

54 Raimi, S, *Spider-Man* (Columbia Pictures, 2002)

55 Favreau, J, *Iron Man* (Marvel Studios, 2008)

56 Branagh, K, *Thor* (Marvel Studios, 2011)

57 Wadlow, J, *Kick-Ass 2* (Universal Pictures, 2013)

Acknowledgements

W riting a book can be a lonely process. It's you and your computer and the internet for hours at a time. However, this time I had the opportunity to speak directly with some of the people who inspire me and my ideas, and who kept me company both in our actual conversations and metaphorically during the long hours of isolation. Special thanks then to Kay Sargent, Jordi Ferrer, L David Marquet, Chris May, Diederick Janse, Cassandra Worthy and Miranda Willems for their contribution to this book.

I'd also like to thank the team at Rethink Press, in particular Sarah Marchant, who offered sensible advice and guidance at various points and then, of course, agreed to publish the book.

Thanks to my clients over the years, many of whom have become friends and have probably helped me grow at least as much as I've helped them.

I could not run my business without my exceptionally organised, patient, warm-hearted and efficient assistant, Stavroula Dimitriou-Fox. She's a mind-reader, always knowing what I need, what the weather is going to be like and which striking union is going to impact my travel plans well before it occurs to me to ask. The same applies to my accountant and the person responsible for the beautiful drawings in this book, Ben Hughes. Not only does he keep me financially responsible, managing the detail that I have such a blind spot for, but he is an incredibly talented artist. His work has brought this book to life. Do look him up at www.benhughesart.co.uk to find out more.

Finally, my daughter Ivy deserves a mention. She has had to listen to me drone on in the car, in the kitchen, early in the morning and late at night, about my latest breakthrough or the struggles I've had that day. She has largely left me alone to get on with it when I've needed to write and has made me laugh so hard some days that I've been begging her to stop. I hope I wasn't too boring.

The Author

Back in the 90s, Blaire was a BBC news journalist, working for flagship Radio 4 programmes like *Today* and *Woman's Hour*. She became fascinated with the new field of leadership coaching and became one of the first professional certified coaches in Europe having left the BBC in 2000. Since then, she's been coaching, provoking and challenging senior leaders and their teams to help them figure out how to lead their organisations in these fast-changing times.

Currently, Blaire speaks internationally at conferences and events, calling on audiences of senior leaders to rethink what leadership means in the twenty-first century. She draws on her experience, all of those private and highly personal conversations, the breakthroughs she's seen extraordinary leaders make and the mistakes she's seen less enlightened leaders make (largely when their egos got in the way of them hearing what they were being told). Increasingly from the stage she's imploring audiences (with, she hopes, a sense of humour and an appreciation of just how hard it is to do what she's asking) to get out of the way of their people and stop being the barrier to those people doing their best work.

These are ideas Blaire's explored in these chapters, but her experience shows that the biggest barrier to change isn't the resistance of junior people. It is the resistance of the most senior people. Unless you do something different, no one else stands a chance.

You can follow Blaire on Instagram:

https://instagram.com/blairepalmercoach

Connect on LinkedIn:

www.linkedin.com/in/blairepalmer

Find out about inviting Blaire to speak at your event:

www.thatpeoplething.com